त्वयैतद्धार्यते विश्वं त्वयैतत् सृज्यते जगत् ।
त्वयैतत् पाल्यते देवि त्वमत्स्यन्ते च सर्वदा ॥ ७५

विसृष्टौ सृष्टिरूपा त्वं स्थितिरूपा च पालने ।
तथा संहृतिरूपान्ते जगतोऽस्य जगन्मये ॥ ७६ ॥

महाविद्या महामाया महामेधा महास्मृतिः ।
महामोहा च भवती महादेवी महासुरी ॥ ७७ ॥

By you this universe is borne, by you this world is created.
By you it is protected, O Devi. By you it is consumed at the end.
You who are eternally the form of the whole world,
at the time of creation you are the form of the creative force,
at the time of preservation you are the form of the protective power,
and at the time of the dissolution of the world
you are the form of the destructive power.
You are the Supreme Knowledge, as well as ignorance,
intellect and contemplation

Devī-Māhātmya

Ajit Mookerjee

KALI

The Feminine Force

with 104 illustrations, 18 in color

DESTINY BOOKS
Rochester, Vermont

In the words of Romain Rolland

To Her,
the Great Goddess,
the invisible, the immanent, who
gathers to her golden arms the
multiform, multicoloured sheaf
of polyphony, to Unity—I dedicate
this new work.

Destiny Books
One Park Street
Rochester, Vermont 05767
www.InnerTraditions.com

Destiny Books is a division of Inner Traditions International

Library of Congress Cataloging-in-Publication Data

Mookerjee, Ajit.
Kālī, the feminine force / by Ajit Mookerjee.
p. cm.
Bibliography : p.
Includes index.
ISBN 0-89281-212-5 (pbk.)
1. Kālī (Hindu deity). I. Title.
BL 1225.K3M66 1988
2954.5'211 - DC19 88-14872
CIP

10 9 8 7 6 5 4

Printed in Hong Kong by
Everbest Printing Co., Ltd.

Frontispiece: Dance of the Great Goddess Kālī.
The yonic triangle represents creation, the breasts represent
preservation, the crown of the head represents reabsorption.
Contemporary expression of traditional form, gouache on paper

Contents

Woman is the creator of the universe,
the universe is her form;
woman is the foundation of the world,
she is the true form of the body.
Whatever form she takes,
whether the form of a man or a woman,
is the superior form.
In woman is the form of all things,
of all that lives and moves in the world.
There is no jewel rarer than woman,
no condition superior to that of a woman.
There is not, nor has been, nor will be
any destiny to equal that of a woman;
there is no kingdom, no wealth,
to be compared with a woman;
there is not, nor has been, nor will be
any holy place like unto a woman.
There is no prayer to equal a woman.
There is not, nor has been, nor will be
any yoga to compare with a woman,
no mystical formula nor asceticism
to match a woman.
There are not, nor have been, nor will be
any riches more valuable than woman.

Śaktisaṅgama Tantra

Acknowledgments

From her transformation after a visit to the Vaiṣno Devī Temple in Jammu-Kashmir, Sudha, my wife, almost in a trance-state, painted the image of Kālī shown on page 2 and on the cover. Since 1957 so many things have happened around this image that they might almost be called a series of miracles. My inspiration to write this book came from this vision, for which I express my deep gratitude to her. I am also indebted to Dr Madhu Khanna for her various suggestions, and to J.R. Bhalla for his help and encouragement, M.C. Joshi, and particularly, to Ajit K. Dutta for his sincere cooperation and for some translations; to Dr K.C. Pandey, on whose English translation of the Krama system of Kashmir Śaivism I have depended for the chapter entitled Supreme Reality; to Swami Jagadiswarananda for his English translation of the *Devī Māhatmyām*; and to Professor Edward J. Thompson and Arthur Marsman Spencer for the English translation of some of Ramprasad's songs; and finally, to the women of the red-light districts of Calcutta, who provided me with an opportunity of listening to their maddening *Śyāmā-saṅgīta*, the devotional songs of Mother Kālī, and Vaishṇava *Padāvalī-kīrtan* songs, keeping alive a great, ancient tradition, for which their names should be written in golden letters.

A.M.

Preface

Kālī manifested herself for the annihilation of demonic male power in order to restore peace and equilibrium. For a long time brutal *āsuric* (demonic) forces had been dominating and oppressing the world. Even the powerful gods were helpless and suffered defeat at their hands. They fled pell-mell in utter humiliation, a state hardly fit for the divine. Finally they prayed in desperation to the Daughter of the Himalayas to save gods and men alike. The gods sent forth their energies as streams of fire, and from these energies emerged the Great Goddess Durgā.

In the great battle to destroy the most arrogant and truculent man-beasts, the goddess Kālī sprang forth from the brow of Durgā to join in the fierce fighting. As the 'forceful' aspect of Durgā, Kālī has been dubbed 'horrific' or 'terrible' in masculine-biased commentaries, without understanding of the episode's inner meaning. The challenge of *śakti* (feminine force) with its vast Śākta literature has not been properly presented to the world from the feminine viewpoint to bring out its truth. Even casual observations on the Durgā episode by a woman writer may give a glimpse of a perspective which has been ignored and distorted by an extreme phallic culture.

'What is there in the story [of Durgā] for us?' writes Léonie Caldecott in 'The Dance of the Woman Warrior'. 'Well, to start with, the fact that the gods could not change their situation themselves, and they had to create a *goddess*, not another god, to do it for them. In a deadlocked situation, *the woman is the only moving element*. Another thing worth noting is that the dualism gods/anti-gods, good/evil, has a lot to do with the deadlock, a fact which is far from irrelevant to the actual cold wars with which military powers play in the world today. That dualism also makes a point of keeping women in their place, making the female condition the undesirable half of the dualistic equation. The only way Durgā can alter the consequences of this division is by employing an adaptability not normally available under the dualistic regime . . .

'Durgā's name means "Beyond Reach". This to me is an echo of the woman warrior's fierce, virginal autonomy. In fact many of the figures associated with her are officially virgin. This is not meant in the limiting sense understood by the patriarchal order, but rather in Esther Harding's sense: she is "one-in-herself", or as Nor Hall puts it, "belonging-to-no-man". More than this, part of the reach she puts herself beyond so adamantly is the reach of society's attempt to describe her to herself. The more repressive the images available to women, the more the virgin condition becomes a defence against these. In extremis, women will reject womanhood itself, if the condition "unable to move around freely", both physically and psychically, is seen necessarily to accompany it.'[1]

Few Western scholars have understood the significance of Kālī. She was derided by early Western writers and missionaries as the patron-goddess of bandits. Phoolan Devi, a contemporary 'Bandit Queen', who suffered rape and humiliation at the hands of the woman-eaters before her violent career was ended, surrendered to the authorities in 1983 beneath a picture of her chosen deity Durgā; her younger sister commented that 'God turns men into saints, but it is men who turn women into dacoits.'[2]

Kālī has been worshipped by saints as well as sinners. Her image today is reproduced by the latest electronic gadgets, and adopted in connection with the women's movement as a symbol to convey their messages. These new appearances in no way diminish the significance of Kālī. On the contrary, if we look deeply into the situation we will find we can explain many phenomena in terms of the same human values.

We have suffered the consequences of unbalanced power for long enough. Our world cannot any longer tolerate the disruption and destruction brought about by demonic force. In the present Kali Age, Kālī is the answer, and she will have to annihilate again in order to reveal the truth of things, which is her mission, and to restore to our natures that divine feminine spirituality which we have lost.

Durgā proceeding to the battle. Pahari school, c. 18th century, gouache on paper

1
Śakti-worship

By you this universe is borne,
By you this world is created,
O Devī, by you it is protected.

Devī-Māhātmya

Śakti means power, force, the feminine energy, for she represents the primal creative principle underlying the cosmos. She is the energizing force of all divinity, of every being and every thing. The whole universe is the manifestation of Śakti. A Śākta, a follower of Śakti-worship, regards her as the Supreme Reality. The ritual side of the Śākta philosophy consists of the worship of the different forms of this Universal Energy personified as a goddess. Śakti is known by the general name *devī*, from the Sanskrit root *div* to shine. She is the Shining One, who is given different names in different places and in different appearances, as the symbol of the life-giving powers of the universe.

India is the only country where the goddess is still widely worshipped today, in a tradition that dates to the Harappan culture of *c.* 3000 BC and earlier. Mother-goddess and fertility cults in which female divinities predominate appear to have constituted the indigenous religious beliefs of the prehistoric period. A prehistoric megalith is still worshipped as the shrine of the Earth Mother, Bolhai, in Madhya Pradesh, Central India. The Goddess is represented by a smooth, oval, red-coated stone. The capstone is about seven feet long, and rings like a bell when struck, or when rubbed with another stone in a ritual still practised. The whole surface has been fashioned without metal tools as a representation of the Earth Mother who is 'the personified abstraction of cosmic life'. She is the first creation, and conceived of as the Great Mother.

In the Kaimur region of Central India archaeologists describe concentric triangles 'where concretionary sandstone and, especially, triangular laminae are set up as shrines for the worship of the female principle, Shakti, which was built by the group of final upper palaeolithic hunters/gatherers'.[3] This Upper Palaeolithic monument

Mother-goddess, c. 2500 BC. Harappa, terracotta

Shrine of the Earth Mother, Bolhai. Megalith, Madhya Pradesh

Earth-goddess plaque, c. 800 BC, from Lauriya-Nandangarh. Gold

is known locally as the Shrine of Kalika Mai (Mother Kālī). Another monument in the same area is the prehistoric Kerai Ki Devī shrine. From Kashmir through the Vindhyan range to South India, monuments dating from as early as 8000 to 2000 BC symbolize 'the great active power in the universe', the feminine principle, Śakti.

In many parts of India megalithic domes and dolmens are built as 'wombs', and their entrances resemble the Great Mother's yonic passage. Cave sanctuaries, too, are identified with the womb of Mother Earth. The Sanskrit word for a sanctuary is *garbha-gṛha*, meaning 'womb-chamber'.

Chalcolithic finds at Bilwali, also in Central India, or at Nevasa, Maharastra, are of Mother-goddess figurines of an 'archaic' type with exaggerated buttocks and heads, noses, arms and breasts. Mother-goddess or Virgin-goddess figurines are also widespread in Mathura, Ahichhatra, Bhita, Kosambi, Kolhapur, Nasik, Ter, Sonepur and Somnath; and we have the Earth-goddess from Lauriya-Nandangarh, and the Goddesses of Abundance of the Śuṅga period (second century BC) and Kuṣhāna period (first to second century AD). Many of the Mother-figures show by wearing and discolouration that through the centuries people have touched their yonic parts, for the genital areas are regarded as the source of all life and focus of the Mother's cosmic energy. The breasts, belly and yonic entrance of the Mother were objects of reverent touch.

Goddess in vessel-shape. Below right, figurine of c. 1500 BC, Bilwali, terracotta. Far right, Kālī-ghaṭa, water-pot symbolizing the goddess's totality, 'pūrṇa' – her self whole and undifferentiated. West Bengal, traditional form

Virgin-goddess and Great Mother (above), Mathura, c. 300 BC, terracotta

Symbols of abundance and the proliferating-power of nature. Yakshī (right), goddess of wealth and guardian of the treasure, 1st to 2nd century AD, ivory. Below, Śrī, goddess of wealth and abundance, 2nd century AD, Mathura, sandstone. Opposite, Śālabhanjikā, a tree-goddess whose sinuous gestures evoke nature's rhythms, AD 800, stone

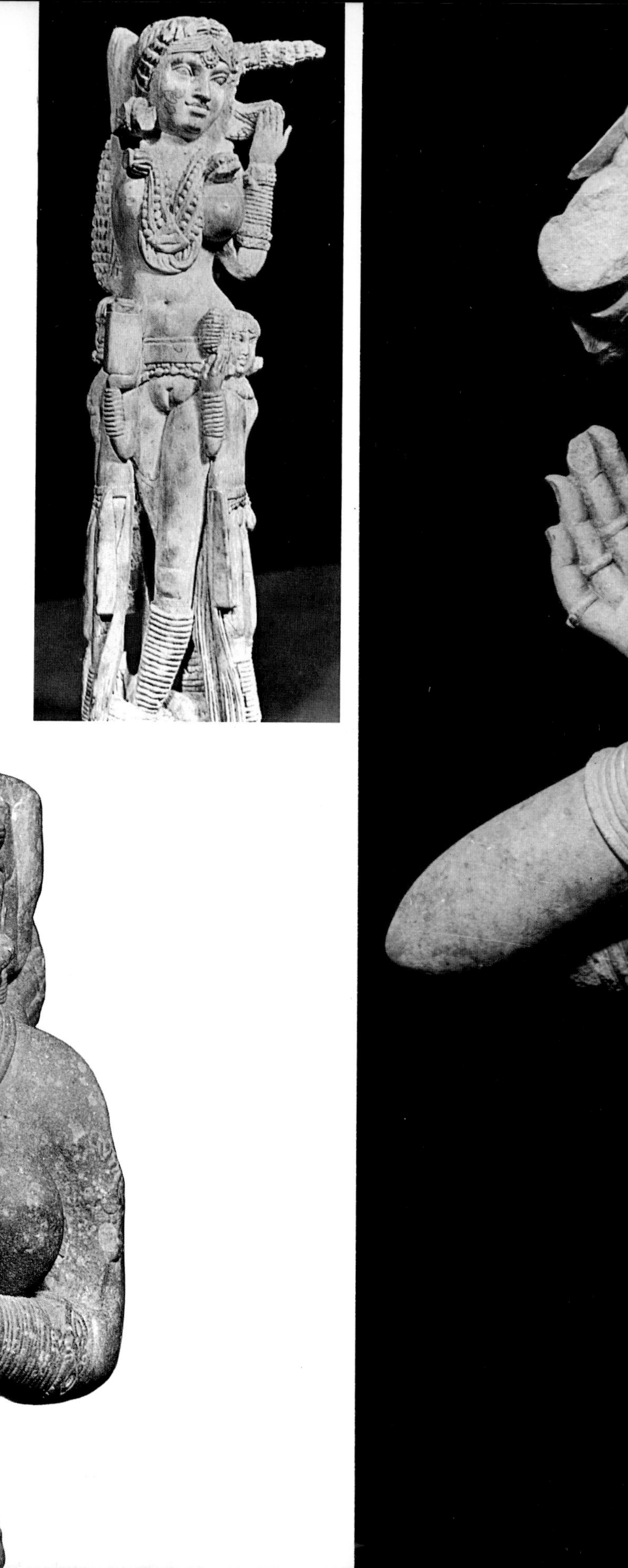

Tree-goddess, 2nd century AD. *Mathura, stone*

From the Navada Toli excavation we have a jar in the form of a nude female figure, dated to the second millennium BC, which represents a Mother-goddess, herself symbolized by the vessel, which is the homologue of the womb. The making of cult vessels is still widespread in India, symbolizing the shaping of life, and rebirth. The vessel itself, as a symbol of the body and fertile womb of the Mother, signifies cyclic recurrence as opposed to the patriarchal view of linear time. Moreover, 'the feminine symbolism of the vessel at its highest level is the vessel of spiritual transformation'.[4]

It is interesting to note the ancient rite by which an Indian prince desiring merit had to enter a large vessel made of gold, a 'golden womb' three cubits high, and that priests performed the ceremonies of *garbhādhāna* (conception) as they would in the case of a pregnant woman. The prince was afterwards taken out of the 'golden womb' and other prescribed rites were performed by the priests as if the prince were a newly born child.[5] A rebirth ceremony is still widely practised, even today, at puberty, when it is known as the rite of '*dvija*', the twice-born – 'born of the womb' and 'born of the rite' – a phenomenon of the maternal creatrix of life. The *Aitareya Brāhmaṇa* prescribes preliminary rites in which the consecrated man, after robing, retires to a hut. There he must remain from sunrise until sunset, and must not be spoken to during that time. He sits curled up with his fists clenched like an embryo. The hut is identified with the womb and the robes with the placenta.[6]

Evidence of feminine ultimacy is widely prevalent in India – whether venerated as Nature or the life-force, as Mother or Virgin, as Great Goddess, or as the Ultimate Reality. As well as the goddess-figurines discovered at the various archaeological sites such as Harappa and Mohenjo-daro, the *Atharva Veda*, which mirrors the way of life and thought of the indigenous peoples (as against the religion of the *Rig Veda*), shows that pre-Vedic, non-Aryan religion and belief were to a great extent female-oriented. Indeed, study of Vedic literature reveals that the feminine divinities popular in the indigenous cults influenced even Vedic religious thought, and that some of these deities were absorbed into the Vedic pantheon.

To set beside the galaxy of powerful female deities which became overwhelmingly popular throughout India in post-Vedic times, the Vedic pantheon had one goddess to compare in importance and influence: Aditi. Aditi is regarded by the Vedic seers as the great womb into which the entire universe has entered. The *Rig Veda*[7] names her as progenetrix of cosmic creation. She holds Agni, god of fire and creator-god, in her womb like a mother. Aditi is the Yoni of the Universe, the Mother-Womb. Almost all the important gods of the Vedic pantheon owe their birth to her.

I *Kālī embodying the energies of creation and dissolution. Nepal. c. 17th century, gouache on paper*

II *Vāc, goddess representing speech and the word, hence associated with creation. Her divinity is recorded in the Rig Veda, c. 1500* BC, *the world's earliest literature. Rajasthan, 17th century, gouache on paper*

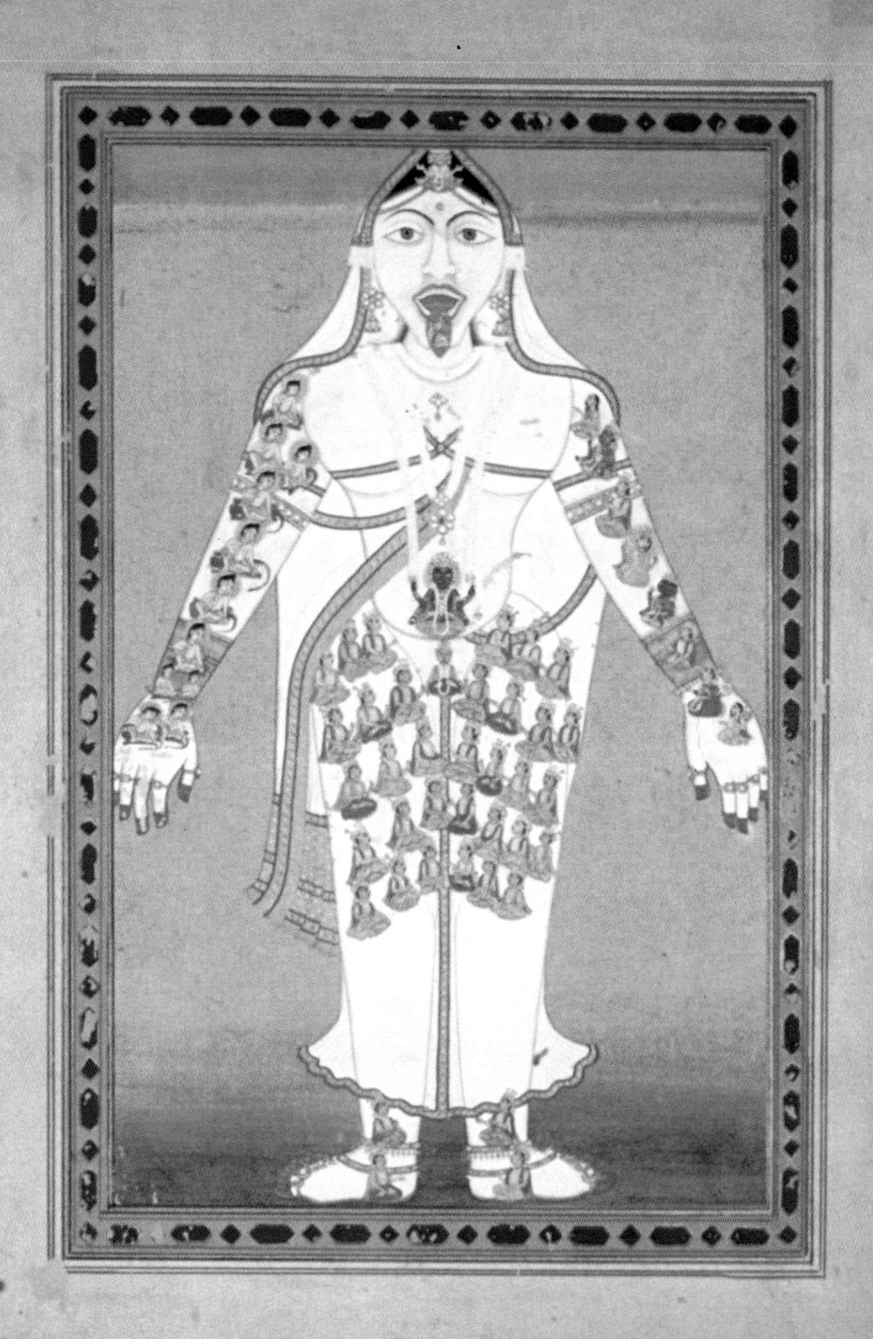

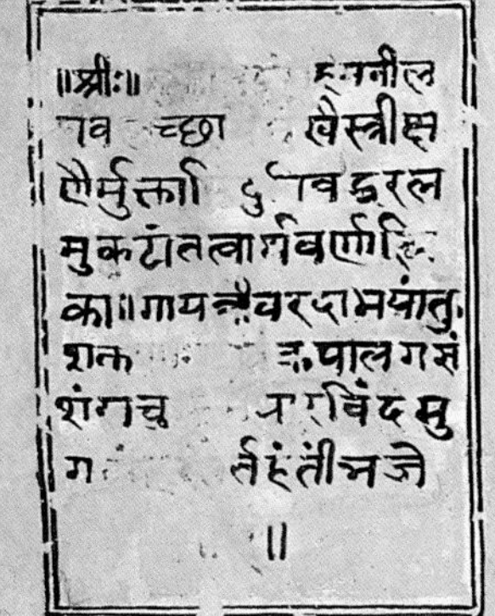

॥श्री॥ विंदु त्रिकोणं पंचा
रषट्कोणं चाष्ट पत्रकं॥
दशपत्र द्वादशारं षोडश
रमतःपरं॥ चतुर्विंशति
पत्रं चतद्वाह्ये भूपुरं तत्रं
॥एवं विलिखितेयंत्रे पू
जयेद्भक्तितत्परः॥ इति
गायत्रीयंत्रोद्धारं चिदंब
ररहस्योतः॥ द॰ नाथूना
रायण चवेंदी सं१९४६ चेत्र
सुदी ३

IV

Aditi has a close nexus with light. She is a shining and luminous Devī. She is also designated law-upholder. Aditi is enumerated among the guardians of *Ṛta*, the Cosmic Order. She is a benevolent and a gentle goddess. In the *Rig Veda*[8] she is offered prayers for humankind's protection. Aditi is the fulfiller of one's desires. She is a mighty deity, and unsurpassed in grandeur. Aditi gives the child happiness, like a mother. She is a household deity. In her bountiful nature Aditi is identified with the cow, for the milk stored in the cosmic cow pours down as our daily nourishment, never exhausted, and circulating as life-substance in all that exists. The Vedic Aditi is already established as the female generative force, and is regarded almost as the Mother-goddess in the Vedic pantheon.

Other goddesses celebrated in the Vedas are Uṣas, the great goddess of dawn; Rātri, the goddess personifying starlit night, who holds such an important place in the Vedic pantheon that a special hymn of the *Rig Veda*[9] is addressed to her as a radiant deity; the goddess of wealth Śrī (Lakshmī), honoured by the *Devī-sūkta* hymn of the *Rig Veda*; Suryā, the Sun-goddess, and Pṛithivī, the Earth-goddess. Other female divinities were looked upon as creative powers. The Vedic Gāyatrī is both a female divinity holding a unique and exalted place and a most sacred mantra. Even today she is venerated, and her mantra is indispensible in any major rite. Vāc (or Saraśvatī) the great goddess of speech or learning, sometimes also a river-goddess, represents the divine energy or śakti inherent in everything – animals, men, gods, the universe. The eight verses of the *Devī-sūkta* hymn[10] which contain this sublime characterization, as well as the *Rātri-sūkta* (hymn to Rātri), occupy a prominent place in the Śākta ritual of later times. The developed Śakti-worship of later days was not a little indebted to the goddess-concepts of the early Vedic age. The very notion of cosmic energy at the root of Śakti of Śāktaism is based on the central theme of the *Devī-sūkta*.[11]

If in the patriarchal framework of the Vedic period the pre-Vedic goddesses to some extent 'went underground', they reappear in post-Vedic literature, and in classical and Medieval Hinduism they regain their former position and importance. The term Śakti is particularly applied to this phase. The Epic and Paurāṇic literature gives innumerable goddess-names to the universal feminine power, and the various goddesses take on distinct iconographic forms. Hundreds of treatises have been written, from *c.* 200 AD to the present day, for the consolidation and development of the Śakti cult. None of the texts of the early period has survived to the present, but our knowledge of them is based on the authoritative philosophical and religious works of the Śākta system from post-Buddhist times to about AD 1200.[12] The term *Tantra* came to be used for such works.

Cosmic Cow. The bull was regarded as subordinate to the cow in the Vedic period. The Rig Veda mentions the cow as 'aghnya', unslayable, while the medieval Purāṇas prescribe cow-worship on three dates during October–November. Rajasthan, 18th century, gouache on paper

III *Gāyatrī, Vedic goddess representing life, energy and creation, whose yantra-diagram unfolds in widening rings of lotus-petals. Rajasthan, c. 18th century, gouache on paper*

IV *Adoration of the Cosmic Cow. In the Medieval (Paurāṇic) period every part of the cow's body is regarded as the abode of a deity, from the nostrils where the Asvins dwell to the tail-tip where Yama, god of death, lies hidden. Nepal, c. 18th century, gouache on cloth*

Top: water-pot wrapped in a red cloth and set on an earth-mound. Traditional rite, Rajasthan

Above: popular representation of Lakshmī, goddess of wealth and fortune. The bindus represent the elements

It is in the Medieval period that a feminine divinity is regarded as the 'power' of her consort-god, and she is often represented as superior to him. In tantric and Śākta doctrine the feminine power (śakti) is supreme, and the gods are virtually relegated to the secondary position. Even the great god Śiva had to use a woman as messenger, when told to do so by the goddess Kālī. She is called Śiva-dūti ('Śiva's female messenger') in an episode of the *Devī-Māhātmya*.[13] In her supreme form Śakti is identified by her worshippers as Mahādevī or Mahāmāyā, the Great Goddess. She is the Power that creates and destroys, the womb from which all things proceed and to which all return. Shrines to the Great Goddess are found throughout the length and breadth of India. She is 'the Mother' or 'Great Mother'.

The Great Mother lives, 'changing, yet changeless', in both classical and popular traditions. At Harappa a nude female figure is represented upside-down with her legs parted and a plant issuing from her yoni. A similar goddess on an early Gupta terracotta seal has legs apart in much the same posture, but a lotus emerges from her neck instead of vegetation from her womb. Such symbolic representations arise from an archetype, although each form carries the imprint of a particular community. The ancient image of vegetation emerging from the body of the goddess reappears in *c.* AD 400 in the *Devī-Māhātmya* where the Devī in her *Śākambharī* aspect is said to nourish her needy people with vegetation produced from her own body. Her body is the earth, source of plant-life and all that lives. As a vegetation goddess, a vital force concerned with growth of crops, the goddess is known as Annapūrṇā, Plenitude of Food, the nourishing sap of all being.

In India today as five thousand years ago, agriculture predominates. Every village has its Mother-goddess and other cult objects, and the majority of *grāma-devatās* (village deities) are feminine. In South India every village has its association with Ammā or Mothers, and their worship is the chief religious practice of the village-priestesses. The villagers among whom Mother-goddesses and fertility goddesses arose continue to centre their religious life on rituals intended to restore the force of the soil, and their earth deities are true vegetation goddesses in the ancient tradition.

Since goddess-rituals handed down from a remote antiquity often centre on the springs of growth and nourishment, many plants are used in goddess-worship. The rite of *Navapatrikā*, for example, includes nine.

The goddess dwelling in a tree or at the water's edge, or in a stone or a shrine, appears under many different names and in many different forms. Sometimes a goddess bears the name of the whole region. Even the vast subcontinent is designated 'Mother India', and the land is

Rādhā and Kṛishṇa, two lovers personifying Nature (Prakṛiti) and Pure Consciousness (Purusha), dual forces sustaining the universe. Kangra school, c. 18th century, gouache on paper

Below: the river goddess Gaṅgā. Bengal, 12th century AD, *stone*

known as *nadīmātṛikā*, 'mothered by rivers'. The goddess is not only the mysterious source of life, she is the very soil, all-creating and all-consuming. She is a power or force which always and everywhere is compelled to manifest and expand itself in the manifold aspects of life.

For the Trika School of Kashmir the feminine creative principle is *Vimarṣa śakti*, 'the world from her womb'. The quality of the life-principle is *spanda* (vibration), according to the *Lakshmī Tantra*. Śakti is spontaneous vibration, the fullness of her blissful state and the outbursting of her joy compelling her towards self-unfolding. 'When Śakti expands or opens herself (*unmiṣhati*), the universe comes into being, and when she gathers or closes herself up (*nimiṣhati*), the universe disappears as a manifestation – an endless phenomenon of her total self "opening" and "closing", bringing into existence countless universes.'[14] The Goddess alternates eternally between a phase of manifestation (*sṛisṭhi*) and dissolution or return to potentiality (*pralaya*); between relative space and time which is curved or circular (*vrittākāra*), and Absolute Space (*svāsvyata-vyom*) and Time, the utter dark depths, Mahākālī. At the time of cosmic dissolution the universe of physical objects is withdrawn again into Śakti, as everything collapses inwards into one dimension: the 'bindu' or seed-state.

Śakti is also known as *Svātantrya*, meaning independence or freedom, because her existence does not depend on anything extraneous to herself, and *Vimarṣa*, meaning being many things at the same time. She is even regarded as substance, because all possible objects are latent and manifest in her womb. 'They have no existence apart from Śakti, and as such are like attributes of this substance'.

In tantric cosmology the whole universe is seen as being built up from and sustained by dual forces, Śakti and Śiva, the feminine and masculine principles; although as Devī says in the *Devībhāgavata*: 'At the time of final dissolution I am neither male, nor female, nor neuter.' 'She' is formless, attributeless, in her ultimate aspect of Reality.

2
Feminine Divinity

Look upon a woman as a goddess
whose special energy she is,
and honour her in that state.

Uttara Tantra

All the pilgrimage-centres exist in woman's body.

Purascharaṇollāsa Tantra

Every entity, feminine or masculine, is a manifestation of Śakti and Śiva, but Śakti is more strongly manifest in the feminine, and Śaktism raises the feminine principle to primacy. It is now known that 'nature's first choice or primal impulse is to [produce] a female'. Genetically speaking, everyone's life is originally female, and 'only when a new substance, the male hormone, is added to the fetus does its gender change'.

In India's cultural diversity the vision of the sacred as woman has never ceased. 'Women are divinity, women are vital breath,' asserts the *Sarvollāsa Tantra*. 'Women are the goddess, women are life. . . . Be ever among women in thought,' it is said the Buddha advised the sage Vaśiṣṭha. Woman is the highest object of devotion. Her dynamic potency brings a vision of the goddess and of the Absolute. As the living embodiment of Śakti, she shares in the creative principle. Her equal participation, even superiority, is essential to tantrism in every one of its aspects.

In the tantric ritual of union called *āsana*, the yoginī or śakti is represented by a living female who epitomizes the entire nature of femaleness, the essence of all the śaktis in their various aspects. Symbolically transformed into a goddess during the course of the ritual, the female partner plays a dynamic role. She 'is', in flesh and blood, the Goddess.

Innate or acquired personal preferences, youth or age, beauty or ugliness, high or low social status, even relationships, have no significance for the ritual of Śaktism. Indeed, the further the mind is removed from the patriarchal standards of feminine beauty, the better. The woman – any woman – represents primordial female in purest form, a personification of totality whose essence makes her archetypal, Jung's anima. When a high-priest and poet of fifteenth-

Cosmic Woman. At her yoni-place is Brahmā, creator; at her breast, Vishṇu, preserver; at her head, Śiva, Pure Consciousness, representing dissolution and reabsorption. Rajasthan, c. 18th century, gouache on paper

Srī Caitanya, born in 1485 in Navadvipa, West Bengal, and venerated during his lifetime as a saint, even as an incarnation of Kṛishṇa. In the last stages of his life he became Rādhā-like – feminine – in his love for the divine. Bengal, c. 18th century, oil on board

Opposite: Devī with the Yoni-maṇḍala for meditation and worship. Himachal Pradesh, c. 17th century, bronze

century Bengal, Chandidas, fell in love with a washer-maid, Rami, against society's strong opposition, he approached his temple deity, the goddess Bāshulī, who told him, 'no deity can offer you what this woman is able to give you'. In another story King Krodha was advised to go to the Yoni-maṇḍala, and to attain salvation by attachment to the *pañca-vesyā*, the five celestial prostitutes.

Moreover it is pronounced that the masculine adept of Śakti-worship becomes 'ideal' if by ritual techniques he can arouse his own feminine quality. It is even suggested he should undergo a process of transvestism (known as *Sakhi-bhāva*, to 'unman men') to attain complete identification with the deity. Ritual transvestism for men is still practised, particularly in Vaishṇavism. Men wear the clothes and ornaments of women, and even observe a few days' monthly retirement-period. According to Vaishṇavite doctrine, 'all souls are feminine to the Supreme Reality'.

Ardhanārīśvara, the deity possessing male and female attributes conjoined, signifies psychic totality. As Ann Belford Ulanov writes in *The Feminine in Jungian Psychology and in Christian Theology*: 'Integration, or spiritual wholeness, is the incarnation and expression of the self which includes and transcends the male-female alternative. Thus Jung reminds us that we cannot attain to spiritual health by neglecting either one of these elements.'[15]

In Śaktism, women and men are not at war, but through their collective uniqueness realize the feminine fullness of the universe. They are the images on earth of the unitary cosmic principle, and in imbalance, they disturb the macrocosmic equilibrium. The two must be one in male-female relationships, in order, as Vivekananda put it, to 'restore the essential balance in the world between the masculine and feminine energies and qualities. The bird of the spirit of humanity cannot fly with one wing.'

'He is She' (Kāmakalāvilasa). Female and male conjoined support and balance the 'Bull of Bulls', Śiva's great animal vehicle (below), symbol of phallic power. Nepal, 18th century, stone.
Right, Ardhanārīśvara, two in one, representing the equilibrium of the feminine and masculine aspects that make up a single human being. Vikrampur (Bangladesh), c. 12th century, stone. For Śaktism, the feminine element is predominant: opposite, hermaphrodite figure, Chola, 11th century, bronze

The rite of yoni-worship. Standing under the arch of a yoginī's legs a devotee drinks 'yoni-tattva', the 'sublime essence'. Madura, c. 17th century, stone

Right: adoration of the yoni, a scene carved below the image of a goddess at the Sixty-four Yoginī Temple, Bheraghat. Madhya Pradesh, 12th century, stone

Opposite: a yoni-shrine, the 16th-century pilgrimage-temple of Kamakhya, Assam. Below, a megalithic 'temple': domed roof over narrow yonic passage leading to an inner chamber. Kerala

The triangle, the yoni-yantra, the immemorial sign of woman, represents the Great Mother as the source of all life, the cosmic womb. The yoni is extolled as a sacred area, the transmission-point for subtle forces, the gateway to cosmic mysteries. In sculptures the goddess is represented lying on her back with legs outspread for worship, or standing with her feet apart while worshippers beneath the arch of her legs drink the *yoni-tattva*, the 'Sublime Essence'. In the *Yonitantra*, the yoni is described as having ten parts, each part connected with a manifestation of the Devī.[16] For the *yoni-pūjā*, or vulva-rite, the vulva of a living woman, or its representation in paint, stone, wood, or metal, is worshipped as a symbol of the goddess.

A famous temple at Kamakhya near Gauhati in Assam is dedicated to yoni-worship. According to the *Purāṇas* and *Tantras*, Śiva became inconsolable at the death of his beloved wife, Satī, and wandered the earth in a mad dance with Satī's dead body on his shoulder. Vishṇu, following Śiva, cut up Satī's body piece by piece to relieve Śiva's burden. Where fragments of her body and limbs fell to earth, fifty-one Śakti-*piṭhas*, pilgrimage-centres, came into existence. Satī's organ of generation fell at Kamakhya, and a temple was built on the hilltop there to mark the spot. It contains no image of the goddess, but in the depths of the shrine there is a yoni-shaped cleft in the rock, adored as the Yoni of Śakti. A natural spring within the cave keeps the cleft moist. During *Ambuvāchi* (July–August), after the first burst of the monsoon, a great ceremony takes place, for the water runs red with iron-oxide, and the ritual drink is symbolic of the *rajas* or *ritu* of the Devī, her menstrual blood. In Kerala a ceremony called

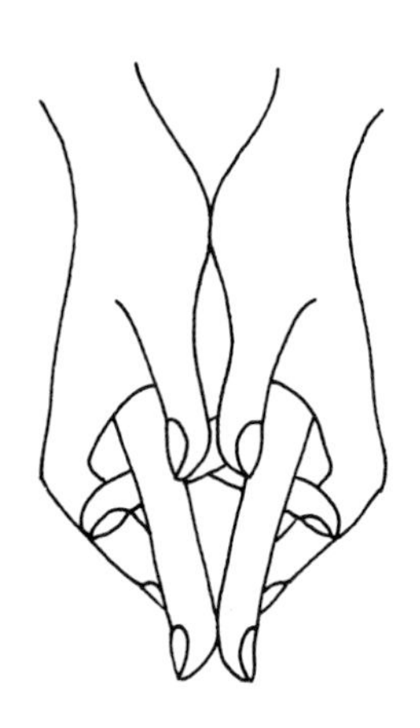

'*trippukharattu*' is held eight or ten times a year. At these periods a reddened cloth wrapped round the image of the goddess is keenly sought after by pilgrims and prized as a holy relic. In other places, rock formations containing natural grottos are regarded as sacred, and the pilgrims are made to crawl through a tunnel representing the birth-canal, and are regarded as born again. Tanks and pools of triangular shape were conceived of as *Yoni-kuṇḍas* (*kuṇḍa* meaning 'of the universe'). Hills with rounded peaks and springs are named *Stana-kuṇḍas* (*stana* meaning 'breast-well'). To bathe in the Yoni-kuṇḍa and to drink the water from the springs sacred to the goddess are popular rites and are considered auspicious.

In Śaktism the menstrual taboo is broken down and the menstrual fluid is regarded as sacred and becomes the object of veneration. A menstruating woman is placed in a special category during ritual practice. Her energy at this time is said to be different in quality, and the rhythm that occurs in her body appears to be related in a mysterious way to the processes of nature. 'At menstruation, when the body passes its blood-food, a woman often feels an ingathering of her energy and feelings to a deeper centre below the threshold of consciousness.'[17] In the *chakra-pūjā* (group ritual-worship) of 'left-hand' tantrikas, menstrual fluid may be taken as a ritual drink along with wine, and a special homage is paid to the yoni, touching it with one's lips and anointing it with sandalwood paste, as the participant offers libation from a yoni-shaped ritual vessel called the *arghya* or *kuśī*.

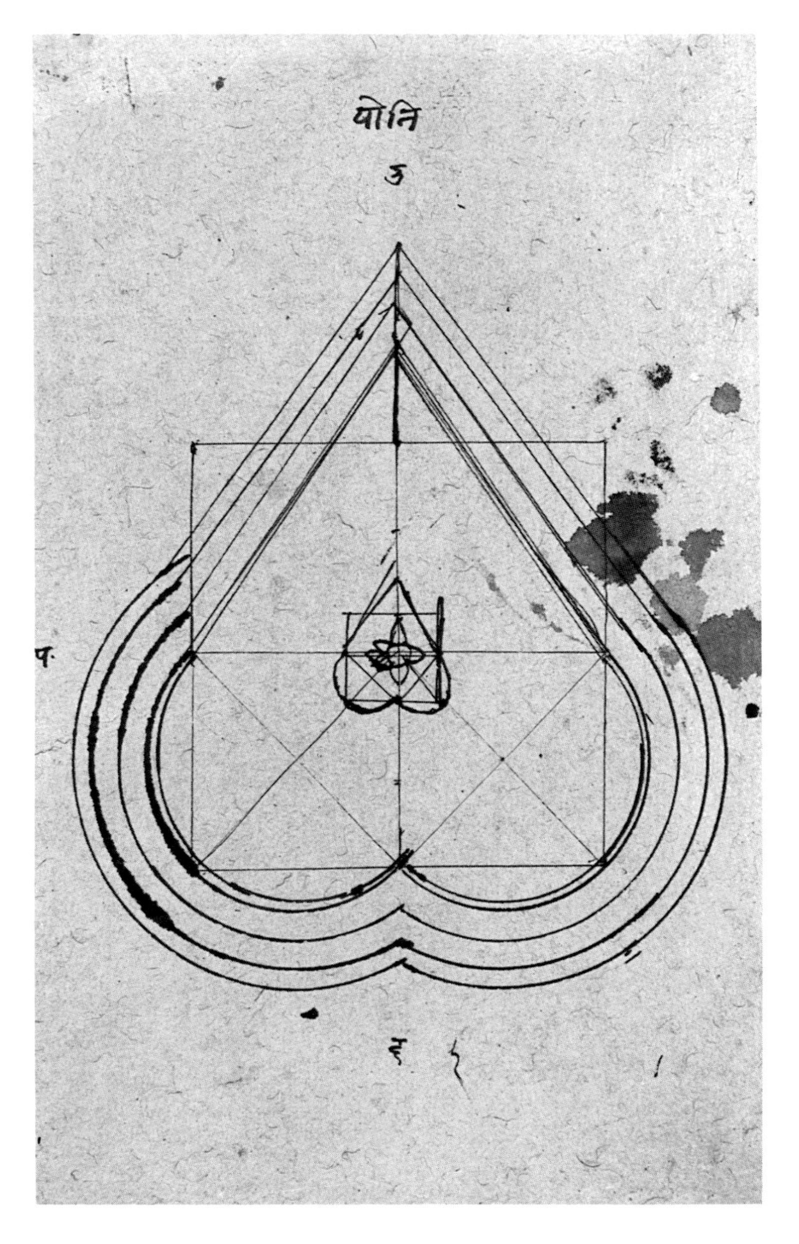

Yoni-kuṇḍa. When the yoni faces the sacrificial altar it becomes 'Urdhvayoni' – the 'erect yoni'. The female triangle points upwards. Opposite, a traditional pool with a crimson-coloured yoni-shape. Left, Urdhvayoni-diagram, Rajasthan, early 19th century, ink on paper. Above, kuśī, a copper vessel used as a holy-water container

Yoni-āsana (opposite, right), the yogic posture symbolizing the womb-source, Rajasthan, c. 18th century, gouache on paper, and Yoni-mudrā (below), the finger-gesture delineating the yonic triangle

In the *Yonitantra* the menstrual flux is designated the 'flower' (*puṣpa*). The Aparājitā-flower has the shape of the yoni, the vulvate shape, and this flower has a specific place in ritual. Similarly the lotus (*padma*) is related to the yoni, and is known as *padma-yoni*. The Great God Brahmā, the Creator, springs from the mysterious lotus arising from the depths of the navel-womb of Vishṇu, linked with Vishṇu by an umbilical cord issuing as a lotus-stalk. Brahmā is known as the Lotus-born. The goddess Lakshmī, Rādhā the consort of Kṛishṇa, and many other deities are associated with the lotus-flower. In Buddhist symbolism, also, the lotus represents the yoni, besides its many other metaphysical meanings.

In identifying a tenth-century Alampur female figure-carving as the goddess 'Aditi-uttānapād', Stella Kramrisch writes: 'Supported by the entire figure, on top of her body is the place of the lotus, the place of the Birth of the Universe. Below, the figure is shown in the physical position of giving birth; above she is herself once more the giver of life, as lotus, the Word that was in the beginning, genetrix of all that exists in the cosmos, genetrix once more of what is manifest as embodied cosmic consciousness.'[18] As another writer observes: 'The

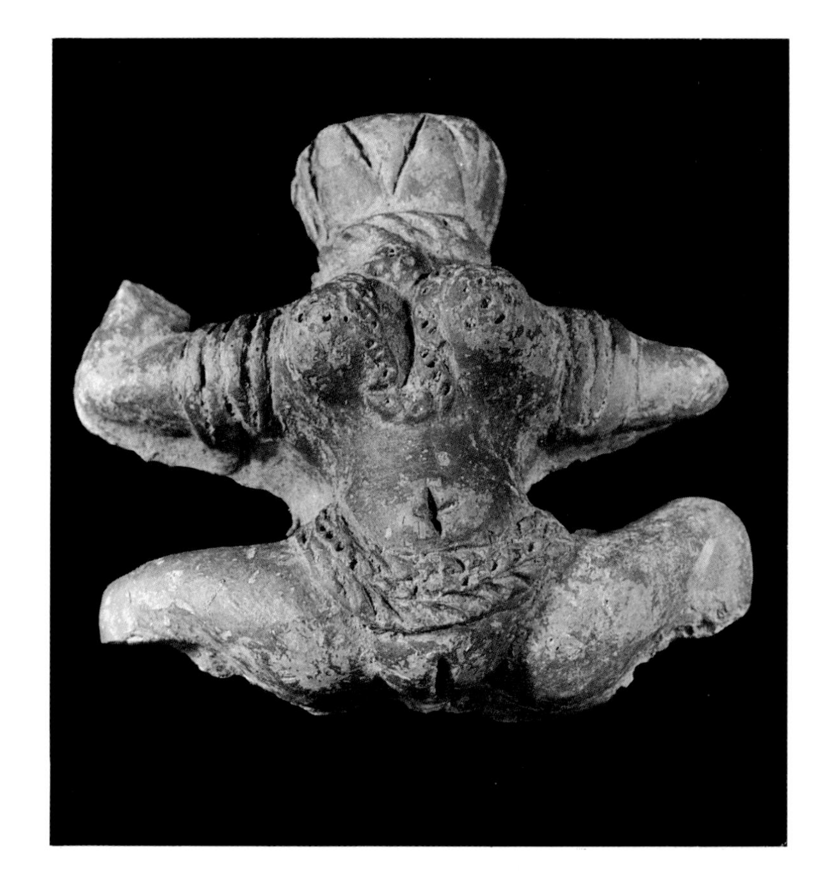

Lotus goddess. The goddess as genetrix of all things, with a lotus-bud emerging from her neck. c. 4th century AD, *terracotta*

Above right: Rati and Kāma, with the feminine Rati in the superior position. Rati represents kinetic energy; the couple's union, utter fullness, completeness. Kangra school, c. 18th century, gouache on paper

Opposite: chart of the energy-centres. According to the Koka Śāstra the eighteen focal points correspond to the phases of the lunar cycle. Rajasthan, c. 17th century, gouache on paper

earth is the first creation; she lies on the lotus, because the lotus has been in India the symbol of creation, the support of all that exists in the material as well as in the spiritual world. In the late hymns, the *Śrīsūkta*, the Earth has become Śrī or Lakshmī – sitting on a lotus, having the colour of the lotus. Just as Śrī and Lakshmī are born from the Ocean (*Mahābhārata*, I, 18, 35, i) so the Earth stands there on the water-born lotus. Waters are the perennial source, the womb of the inexhaustible possibilities of existence; creation is the first appearance of a lotus-flower.'[19]

The lotus represents the perfection of beauty and symmetry. The yoni is likened to the lotus in the early stage of its opening and in its fully open form. Like the lotus which is not saturated by the water that it rests upon, any more than its flowers are soiled by mud, the yoni remains perpetually pure and is not soiled by any action.

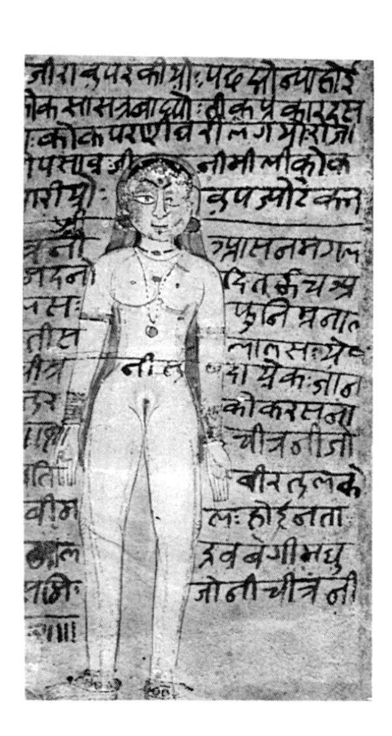

The monthly efflorescence of woman in her cycle in rhythm with the lunar cycle creates a body-consciousness which is related to the processes of the universe. Since, according to tantra, the body is the link between the terrestrial world and the cosmos, the body is, as it were, the theatre in which the psycho-cosmic drama is enacted. Tantric literature records an extensive body-language, usually known as the science of *Amṛitakalā* (*kalā* meaning fraction), which charts the energizing centres of the female body according to the calendar of the light and dark halves of the moon, the Chandrakalā (moon-fraction). Woman's body is both a unity and an organism directed towards oneness, wholeness.

The spread of the Śakti cult stimulated an awareness of woman's autonomous freedom. In the thirteenth century, one commentator on

Rādhā reproaching Kṛishṇa. Kangra school, c. 18th century, gouache and gold on paper

V The 'Lotus World'. The lotus is the symbol of manifestation. Kṛishṇa (Purusha) is seen as separate, detached, because of his knowledge: 'She is Śakti. Hladini (Beauty of the World) is seen by me.' Rādhā (Śakti, Prakṛiti) is separate because of her knowledge: 'I am seen.' Where there is no longer duality for the sake of creation, there is total Unity. Basohli school, c. 18th century, gouache on paper

VI Devotees wearing Kālī's colour, the red of energy, for the festival procession to the Bhagavata (Kālī) Temple, Kerala

Vatsyayana's *Kāmasūtra* even states that a woman's virtue can be judged in relation to the number of lovers she has had. The twentieth-century poet Rabindranath Tagore writes that 'a thousand years' effort is worthwhile to win a woman's heart'. The triumph of Śakti is described in spectacular myths and legends, and gave birth to a new iconography in Indian art, glorifying the feminine.

In the *Gandharva Tantra* it is written that 'She who is Sun, Moon and Fire, and half of Ha [Śiva], lays down the Purusha [the male principle] and enjoys him from above.' The *Niruttara Tantra* states that 'when *nirguṇa* [attributeless] Kālī becomes *saguṇa* [manifest] she is engaged in *viparīta-rati* [sexual union with the female partner in the superior position] while Śiva is the passive one. It is she who has brought the universe into existence . . . If Śiva is united with Śakti, he is able to exert his powers as lord; if not, the god is not able to stir.'

V

Śakti of the Śāktas is not the consort of Śiva. In her cosmic self, Śakti-Śiva are eternally conjoined. The significance of *viparīta-rati* in the copulative cosmogony is of the feminine principle constantly aspiring to unite, the feminine urge to create unity from duality, whereas the masculine principle, with each thrust, invariably separates, representing the phase of dissolution of the universe.

Mahākālī, an 'annihilation' aspect of Śakti, is depicted standing upon the recumbent couple Kāma and Rati, with the feminine Rati in the active role in which the female straddles the male. Kālī is also known as Vāmā, 'she who is on the left'. The *Nirvāṇa Tantra* says that 'Vāmā is the granter of Great Liberation after conquering *Dakshiṇa* [Śiva who is on the right].' The left, female, conquers the right, male, hence the goddess is called Dakshiṇa-Kālī. As James Joyce warns in *Ulysses*: '. . . beware of the left, the cult of Shakti'. The *Kubjikā Tantra* asserts: 'Not Brahmā but Brahmānī [feminine] creates; it is Vaiṣnavī, not Vishṇu who protects; Rudrānī, not Rudra [Śiva] who takes all things back.' The energy of god is feminine, and every god is static, even dead, without his śakti. Śiva says to Durgā in the *Bramavaivarta Purāṇa*: 'I, the Lord of All, am a corpse without you,' and Kṛishṇa confesses to Rādhā: 'Without you I am lifeless in all actions.' Devī Tripurasundarī is represented as reclining on a couch supported by five inert gods, Sadāśiva, Iśāna, Rudra, Vishṇu and Brahmā.

'The male form, the female form, any form – all forms are undoubtedly Her Supreme Form,' says the *Gandharva Tantra*. Even the powerful gods crave to enter feminine form. Vishṇu had to transform himself into a female as Mohinī, who entranced and almost seduced Śiva. Śiva as Bhairava took on many aspects of Kālī. The transformation of male to female is narrated in the legends of many Purāṇas. In one of such stories, King Īla, while hunting, came upon a grove where Śiva was making love with Pārvati and had taken the form of a woman to please her. Everything in the woods, even the trees, had become female, and as he approached, King Īla was turned into a woman. Śiva, laughing, told him he could 'ask for any boon except masculinity'. In some temples Śiva's powerful bull-vehicle, Nandi Bull, is portrayed almost as if it were a feminine deity. Approaching Śiva and his bull-vehicle, a worshipper will step upon a masculine outline laid into the floor – a symbolic shedding of the egocentric male outlook.

The feminine power has been given expression in a multitude of female figures, both in sculpture and in painting, in which the emphasized forms of breasts, belly, hips, yoni and thighs seem an incarnation of the rhythms of the universe. From the Medieval period, tantra's bold depictions of the themes of sexual union, menstruation, pregnancy and childbirth restored to sacred art essential symbolic figurations virtually suppressed by taboo.

VII *Male devotee dressed as Bhagavatī or Vāgeśvanī, a manifestation of Kālī in tiger-form. Cheruvathur Muchilot Temple, near Payyanur, Kerala*

VIII *Nandi Bull, Śiva's powerful vehicle. Jejuri, c. 17th century, brass*

IX *Masculine shape set into the pathway leading to the temple's inner chamber. Jejuri, c. 17th century*

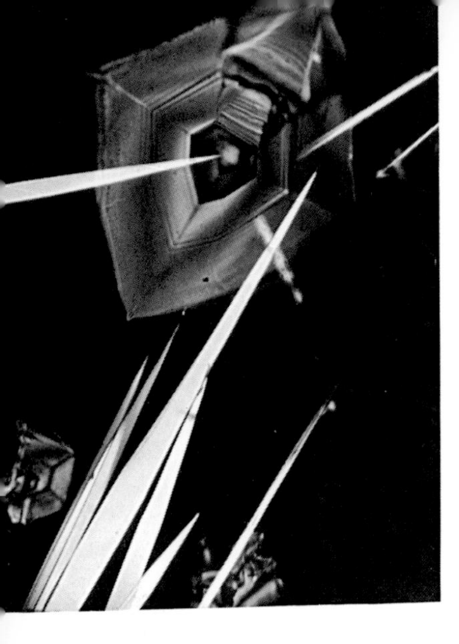

Female hormone, a yonic shape. Photograph by Lennart Nilsson

Menstruation. For tantra, the human body is the microcosm, the theatre in which the psycho-cosmic drama is enacted. In the Yonitantra the menstrual flux is designated the 'flower' – puṣpa. South India, c. 18th century, wood

Conception. A mighty force is striving towards differentiation, manifestation. Uttar Pradesh, c. 17th century, gouache on paper

Pregnancy. Kaumārī, 'Power-of-youth', one of the Sapta Mātṛikā, the Śakti's known as the Seven Divine Mothers. Her belly signifies the universal phase of preservation. Rajasthan, 6th century AD, chlorite schist

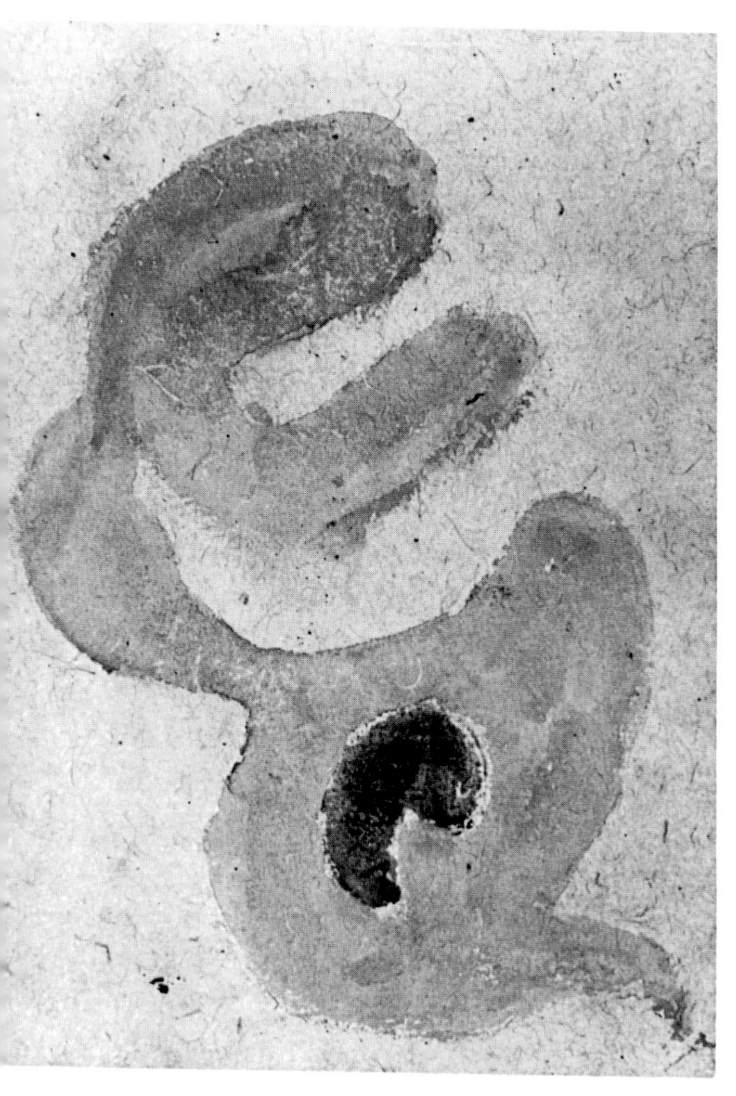

Birth. The Great God Vishṇu becomes incarnate as Kṛishṇa through the womb. Not even the gods are exempt from the birth-process. Folk-painting, Birbhum, West Bengal, c. 18th century, gouache on paper

Below: human birth symbolizing the universal phase of creation. South India, c. 18th century, wood

Opposite: Motherhood, exemplified by Yaśoda and the child Kṛishṇa. Karnataka, c. 16th century, copper

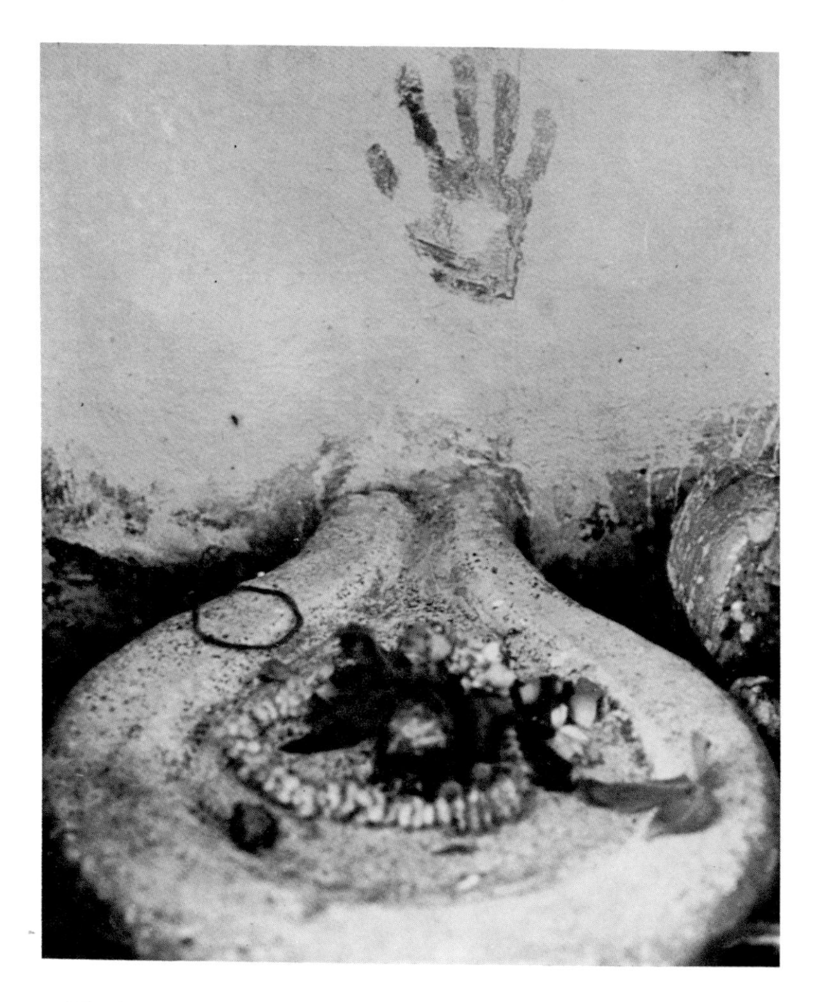

Opposite: the feminine as the embodiment of Śakti, the rhythmical forms pointing to the 'root of bliss'. Uttar Pradesh, c. 5th century, red sandstone

Yoni-liṅga shrine. Rajasthan, traditional form. Below: Liṅga-yoni. Kangra school, 18th century, gouache on paper

The image of the liṅga-yoni does not, as is commonly suggested, convey the power of the active masculine principle by representing the penetration of the liṅga into the yoni. To the contrary, as Stella Kramrisch has pointed out, 'the abstract geometrical shape . . . of the *urdhvaliṇga* [erect phallus] . . . placed on the yoni as its pedestal, rises out of the *yoni*, the womb; it does not enter it. The *liṅga* in the *yoni* emerges from the *yoni* . . .'.[20] This fundamental relationship of liṅga and yoni has been obscured by patriarchal interpretation, yet the emphasis on liṅga-worship could not suppress the widespread rituals surrounding the ever-creative yoni. For the goddess is the matrix of all that exists: whatever is, in the world of things, from Brahman (the Ultimate Reality) to a blade of grass, owes her its origin and is dependent upon her.

The development of the pan-Indian Śakti movement, from its deep and ancient roots to its present-day expansion, is a great nonviolent resurgence of the feminine spirit such as the world has never seen.

3
Feminine Force

Those Thy lovely forms
in the Three Worlds,
And those Thy furious forms,
Save us in all of them.

Devī-Māhātmya

The Great Goddess Durgā was born from the energies of the male divinities when the gods became impotent in the long-drawn-out battle with the *asuras*. All the energies of the gods united and became supernova, throwing out flames in all directions. Then that unique light, pervading the Three Worlds with its lustre, combined into one, and became a female form.

The Devī projected an overwhelming omnipotence. The three-eyed goddess was adorned with the crescent moon. Her multiple arms held auspicious weapons and emblems, jewels and ornaments, garments and utensils, garlands and rosaries of beads, all offered by the gods. With her golden body blazing with the splendour of a thousand suns, seated on her lion or tiger vehicle, Durgā is one of the most spectacular of all personifications of Cosmic Energy.[21]

A tremendous power is poised ready for the grim battle to wipe out demonic forces, the *asuras* whose exaggerated ego-sense is destroying the balance of the universe, and whose sole purpose is to dominate and control. It is the universal war between knowledge and ignorance, truth and falsehood, the oppressor and the oppressed.

The world shook and the seas trembled as the goddess engaged the Great Demon Mahiṣāsura and his hosts in fierce battle, creating her own female battalions from her sighs breathed during the fighting. When the battle was over, the Devī had destroyed the demon's army, symbolic of disruptive aggression

Enraged by her victory, Mahiṣāsura took on buffalo-form to overcome the goddess. Repeatedly the goddess slew the buffalo-demon, and each time he transformed himself into a new and more ferocious shape. Then, with the strength of spiritual energy gained by drinking from the wine-cup charged with spiritual force, the goddess struck the demon-head from the buffalo-body. The chief demon

Durgā vanquishing the Great Demon. Orissa, stone

Mahiṣāsura was dead, and the gods praised the goddess, joyfully worshipping her with flowers, incense and fragrant paste:

Thou Ambikā [a name of Durgā] dost overspread the universe with Thy power.
The power of all divine beings is drawn into Thy form.
Thou art Great Mother, worshipped by all divine beings and sages.
We bow ourselves in devotion to Thee.
Bless us with all that is good for us.

We bow before Thee, O Devī,
Thou who art the good fortune of the virtuous,
Ill-fortune in the house of the evil,
Intelligence in the minds of the learned,
Faith in the hearts of the good,
The modesty of the high-born.

O Caṇḍikā, none can speak of Thy power and might,
Not even Brahmā, Vishṇu, Śiva and Ananta.
Send us Thy thoughts for the protection of the universe
And for the uprooting of all dangers.
Thou whose nature it is to subdue the wicked,
Whose beauty is beyond imagining,
Whose power destroys those who rendered the devas powerless,
Compassionate even towards those enemies . . .

Those Thy lovely forms in the Three Worlds
And those Thy furious forms,
Save us in all of them.

But this victory was not the end of the episode. Two other powerful asuras, Śumbha and Niśumbha, had deprived the gods of their divine functions, and once more the gods prayed to the goddess:

Thou who art terrible,
Thou who art eternal . . .
Thou who art the moon and the moon's light
And happiness itself . . .

The goddess as Pārvati did not yield at once to this masculine adoration. Instead, she projected her feminine psyche from her body, personified as Kauśiki, the 'sheathed one', to enable her to evaluate their prayers in her own 'shadow-self'. Being convinced, she projected

The goddess Durgā defeats the asuras' army and puts it to flight. Kangra school, c. 18th century, gouache on paper. Below: Durgā overcomes Mahisāsura, the Great Demon, in the shape of elephant, and (right) strikes the demon head from the buffalo-body

Caṇḍa and Muṇḍa find the Devī seated upon the mountainside

an overwhelming omnipotence. As Kālikā she stationed herself on Mount Himalaya.

There Caṇḍa and Muṇḍa, servants of the powerful demons Śumbha and Niśumbha, came upon Ambikā bearing a surpassingly charming form. They returned and told Śumbha: 'O King, a most beautiful woman dwells there, shedding a radiance on Mount Himalaya. Never has such beauty been seen. Find out who the goddess is, O Lord, and take possession of her. A jewel, of exquisite limbs, illumining the four quarters with her lustre, O Lord of Demons. All the precious gems, the elephants, horses, and treasures of the Three Worlds have been brought together in your house. . . . Why is this beautiful jewel of a woman not seized by you?'

This time the goddess was met, not with confrontation, but with the masculine tactics of seduction, to disarm her with flattery. Śumbha sent the great demon Sugrīva to the Devī to win her, commanding him: tell her this, and this, speak to her in such a manner that she will quickly come to me in love. The messenger went to the beautiful place in the mountains where the Devī was staying and spoke sweet words to her: 'O Devī, Śumbha Lord of Demons is sovereign over the Three Worlds. Lend your ear to the words of him whose command is never resisted by the devas, and who has vanquished all the demons' foes: "The Three Worlds are mine, and the gods obey me. . . . All the choicest gems in the Three Worlds are mine. O beautiful lady, jewel of womankind, come to us, for we are enjoyers of the best. Come to me, and to my valiant younger brother Niśumbha. Wealth beyond compare will be yours by marrying me. Reflect upon this, and become my wife."'

The Devī replied serenely: 'What you say is true. Śumbha is indeed sovereign of the Three Worlds, and so is Niśumbha. But how shall what I have promised be made false? Hear the promise I have made to myself, in my foolishness. He who conquers me in battle, who removes my pride, who is my match for strength here in the world, he shall be my husband. So let Śumbha come here, or the great asura Niśumbha. Let him vanquish me here, and he may soon claim my hand in marriage.'

'O Devī,' answered the messenger, 'you are haughty, do not speak so. What man in the Three Worlds can stand out against Śumbha and Niśumbha? Not even Indra and all the gods can withstand the asuras in battle. How should you, a woman, stand against them? Take my advice, and go to Śumbha and Niśumbha; do not lose your dignity by being dragged to them by your hair.'

The Devī answered: 'It is true. Śumbha is strong, and Niśumbha is exceedingly valiant: but what can I do, since my unthinking vow was taken long ago?'

Devī prepares to destroy the Demon-chief with the syllable 'Huṃ'

The messenger returned, filled with indignation, and related to the Demon King what the Devī had said. The King, enraged, ordered his army chieftain to 'make haste to bring this shrew to me by force. Drag her to me by the hair.'

Finding the goddess standing on the snowy mountainside the chieftain ordered her to come to Śumbha and Niśumbha. 'If you will not come to my lords now with pleasure, I shall take you by force, and in distress as you are dragged by your hair.' The Devī answered that, since the chieftain came accompanied by an army, 'If you will take me by force, what can I do?' The demon-chief thereupon rushed forward.

Ambikā reduced him to ashes with a mere sound, a supersonic *Huṃ*, while her spirited and angry lion destroyed the asuras' army.

When Śumbha learned that his chief and army had been destroyed he commanded his servants Caṇḍa and Muṇḍa to go with a large force to bring the Devī to him speedily, dragging her by the hair, injured or in fetters if need be.

Fully armed and led by Caṇḍa and Muṇḍa, the asuras marched to where the Devī, smiling gently, was seated upon her lion on a high golden peak of the mountain. Upon seeing her, some of the demons excitedly tried to capture her, while others approached her with their bows bent and swords drawn.

Thereupon Ambikā became terrible in her anger, and her countenance darkened until it was black as ink. From her frowning forehead issued the awesome goddess Kālī, armed with a sword and a noose. Holding a skull-topped staff, skull-garlanded, wrapped in a tiger-skin, emaciated, wide-mouthed, lolling-tongued, with deep-sunken red eyes, Kālī filled the skies with her roar. Laughing terribly, she devoured the demon army, flinging the elephants into her mouth along with their riders, crunching-up chariots and horses with her teeth, crushing others with her feet, striking with her sword and beating with her staff, until the army was laid low.

The great demon Caṇḍa unleashed a hail of arrows and Muṇḍa hurled discuses by the thousand, hiding the fierce Devī until they vanished into her mouth. At this, Kālī, roaring frightfully, her sharp teeth gleaming, laughed with intense rage. Mounting her great lion she rushed at Caṇḍa, and seizing him by the hair, severed his head with her sword. Seeing Caṇḍa cut down Muṇḍa next rushed towards her. She felled him to the ground, striking with her sword in fury. With the brave Caṇḍa and Muṇḍa fallen the rest of the army fled in all directions. Kālī carried the heads to Durgā, saying: 'I bring you the heads of Caṇḍa and Muṇḍa, two great animal-offerings in this sacrifice of battle. Śumbha and Niśumbha you yourself shall kill.' Durgā told Kālī she would be known by the name Cāmuṇḍā, 'because you have brought me Caṇḍa and Muṇḍa'.

Black Kālī issues from the brow of Durgā to join the battle, tossing the asuras into her mouth, filling the skies with her roar

Kālī as Cāmuṇḍā: 'she who brings Caṇḍa and Muṇḍa'

Śumbha himself now set out against the Devī with even larger numbers. Hearing the army advancing, Caṇḍikā (Durgā) made a mighty sound, plucking her bow-string and ringing her bell. The lion roared. Kālī filled the four quarters with the syllable *Huṃ*. Śaktis (energies) of all the gods emanated from their bodies, armed with weapons and mounted for the battle. The Devī appointed a woman to be a messenger between Śiva and the demons. Then the army was pierced through, slashed, put to flight with holy water, pursued as it fled by the violent laughter of Śiva.

The mighty demon Raktabīja remained. From the blood shed from his wounds sprang thousands of fresh combattants, representing the destructive masculine principle. To annihilate this archetypal power, Kālī again and again drank the *rakta-bīja* (the 'seed-blood'). This symbolic devouring represents the 'taking-possession-of' or rendering harmless of an overpowering destructive element, a phallic power.

An even more terrible army advances against the devīs

Following this dreadful battle, the Devī slew the demon Niśumbha. Finding his brother was dead, Śumbha said to the goddess: 'O Durgā, you are puffed up with pride in your strength, but don't show your pride to me. You are exceedingly haughty, but you resort to others' strength to fight.'

Taunted by Śumbha for battling with the strength of her female host, Durgā did not fall into the trap. She drew the multiple forms of the female divinities into her nourishing breasts, into her mothering womb, exercising the powers of protection and preservation without which she would not be the feminine. The Devī answered: 'The many forms that I projected by my own powers are withdrawn into myself. Here I stand alone. Now fight steadfastly.'

Goddess and Demon fought first with their weapons and then hand-to-hand in close combat. Seizing the Devī, Śumbha sprang up and mounted high into the sky. In a 'star wars' battle, Śumbha and Caṇḍika fought as never before, astonishing the *Siddhas* and the sages, until at last Śumbha fell, pierced by her dart.

All the gods, led by Agni, their objective gained and their faces radiant with joy, praised the goddess:

Salutation, O Nārāyanī.
Thine is the power of creation, preservation and dissolution.
Thou art eternal. Thou art the Ground of Being.
Thou art the energies of Nature.

Durgā confronts Śumbha, her Śaktis withdrawn into her own body

Salutation, O Nārāyanī,
Thou who workest the salvation of those in suffering and distress who take refuge in Thee.
Thou, O Devī, who removes the sufferings of all . . .

Who is there but Thyself in the sciences,
in the Scriptures, and in the Vedic sayings
that light the lamp of understanding.

O Queen of the universe, protector of the universe, support of the universe.
Thou art the goddess worthy to be adored by the Lord of the universe.
Those who bow to Thee in devotion become the refuge of the universe.

O Devī, be Thou pleased, and grant us protection from the fear of foes forever,
as Thou hast protected us now by the destruction of the asuras.
Destroy the sins of all the worlds and the great calamities that have arisen through the maturing of evil portents.

The world was at peace again. The skies cleared, the rivers kept their courses, there was sweet singing and dancing. The winds blew

The gods' powers restored, Durgā receives their joyful salutations (top). Her purpose fulfilled and the world once more at peace, she departs, never to return until such time as her divine force is once again needed

softly, the sun shone brilliantly, the sacred fires burned steadily. Strange sounds that had arisen in the various quarters died away.

The departing Durgā offered the gods a boon. She promised that as *Śākambharī* she would nourish the world in time of need with the vegetation grown from her own body, and that in her 'terrible' form she would deliver her worshippers from their enemies, and bless them. Then she vanished from the very spot on which the gods were gazing.

As Esther Harding observed of 'The Virgin Goddess', it can be said of Durgā here that: 'Her divine power does not depend on her relation to a husband-god, and thus her actions are not dependent on the need to conciliate such a one or to accord with his qualities and attitudes. For she bears her identity through her own right.'[22]

The disappearance of Durgā from the battlefield after the victory over aggression expressed one of the deepest truths of the episode, for the feminine action in the cosmic drama is without retentive, ego-seeking ambition.

Durgā depicted with seven hundred verses in her praise (known as the Durgā-Saptasati or Caṇḍi-pāṭha, popularly, Caṇḍi) that are chanted one hundred times during the five days of her annual festival. Rajasthan, c. 18th century, gouache on paper

Durgā is linked with some of the oldest known prayers for humankind's protection: the *Durgā* and *Sāvitrī* of the *Taittereya Āranyaka*, the *Durgā-stotra* or prayer of Yudhiṣṭhira in the *Mahābhārata*. According to the *Brahmavaivarta Purāṇa* Kṛishṇa worshipped Durgā in Goloka, the cow-realm of his youth. Śiva invoked Durgā when confronted by the demon Tripura; Brahmā worshipped her when attacked by two demons Madhu and Kaitabha; and Indra when cursed by Durvāśā. In the *Harivaṁsa*, King Pradyumṇa prays to the goddess for victory over the demon Sambara.

The goddess's several names in the *Devī-Māhātmya* (Caṇḍikā, Ambikā, Cāmuṇḍā, etc.) refer to her qualities and functions. An abundance of names witnesses to the numerous manifestations of divine power, according to the *Bṛhaddevatā*, written toward the fifth century BC, where, however, it is the goddess Vāc who has many names, including Durgā and Gauri. The goddess's oldest names, Ambikā and Umā, continue in use to the present time.

4
Manifestations of Kālī

Thou art the seed of the universe,
And the supreme Māyā.
All this universe has been bewitched by Thee.
Thou, when pleased, art the cause of
salvation to human beings.

Devī-Māhātmya

Kālī, one of the most intoxicating personifications of primal energy in the cosmic drama, gained an extraordinary popularity in Śaktism and is the object of fervent devotion in tantric forms of worship. She is a power-symbol embodying the unity of the transcendental. As we have seen, she makes her 'official' début *c.* AD 400 in the *Devī-Māhātmya*,[23] where she is said to have emanated from the brow of Durgā during one of the battles between the divine and anti-divine forces. In this context Kālī is considered the 'forceful' form of the Great Goddess Durgā.

In Mahākālī (the Great Kālī of the *Devī-Māhātmya*) there is an overwhelming intensity, a mighty strength, a force to shatter all obstacles. She is there for swiftness, for immediate and effective action, for the direct stroke, the frontal assault that carries everything before it. Awe-inspiring, determined and ruthless, she destroys evil force.

At the moment when Kālī sprang forth as the Primordial Śakti we are told that she filled the skies with her roar. This is not, as some commentators have suggested, to be interpreted as a 'savage cry'. As C.G. Jung has pointed out, 'the impact of an archetype, whether it takes the form of immediate experience or is expressed through the spoken word, stirs us because it summons up a voice that is stronger than our own. Whoever speaks in primordial images speaks with a thousand voices . . .'.[24]

The name Kālī has been used generically from antiquity. It has been the practice in India to attribute the achievements of one goddess to another. The idea is that the different manifestations are for a certain definite purpose, and in reality there is one Devī who assumes various forms to fulfil various purposes. Sometimes she assumes a frightening form and sometimes a benevolent form.

Folk-painting of the dancing Kālī. Orissa, contemporary version of traditional form, colours on lacquered cloth

Image of Kālī encircled by purifying flames, AD 1000, Malangi, gilt-bronze

Smashānakālī in union with Śiva. Rajasthan, 18th century, brass

Kālī's fierce appearances have been the subject of extensive descriptions in several earlier and later tantric works. She is most commonly worshipped nowadays as Dakshiṇakālī – the south-facing, black Kālī. Though her fierce form is filled with awe-inspiring symbols, their real meaning is not what it first appears – they have equivocal significance.

The image of Kālī is generally represented as black: 'just as all colours disappear in black, so all names and forms disappear in her' (*Mahānirvāṇa Tantra*). In tantric rituals she is described as garbed in space, sky-clad (*digaṃbarī*). In her absolute, primordial nakedness she is free from all covering of illusion. She is Nature (Prakṛiti), stripped of 'clothes'. She is full-breasted; her motherhood is a ceaseless creation. She gives birth to the cosmos parthenogenetically, as she contains the male principle within herself. Her dishevelled hair (*elokeshī*) forms a curtain of illusion, the fabric of space-time which organizes matter out of the chaotic sea of quantum-foam. Her garland of fifty human heads, each representing one of the fifty letters of the Sanskrit alphabet, symbolizes the repository of knowledge and wisdom, and also represents the fifty fundamental vibrations in the universe. She wears a girdle of human hands – hands are the principal instruments of work and so signify the action of karma or accumulated deeds, constantly reminding us that ultimate freedom is to be attained as the fruit of karmic action. Her three eyes indicate the past, present and future. Her white teeth, symbolic of *sattva*, the translucent intelligence stuff, hold back her lolling tongue which is red, representing *rajas*, the activating quality of nature leading downwards to *tamas*, inertia. Kālī has four hands (or, occasionally, two, six, or eight). One left hand holds a severed head, indicating the annihilation of ego-bound evil force, and the other carries the sword of physical extermination with which she cuts the thread of bondage. One right hand gestures to dispel fear and the other exhorts to spiritual strength. In this form she is changeless, limitless primordial power, acting in the great drama, awakening the unmanifest Śiva beneath her feet.

Black Kālī is worshipped in cremation grounds as Smashānakālī. She makes her abode there to receive those who come to take rest in her.

As Virgin-creator, Kālī is depicted as *sattva-guṇa*, white;[25] as sustaining Mother, *rajas*, red; as the Absorber of all, *tamas*, black. In the equilibrium of the potential state there will always be disturbance arising from the desire for creation – a cycle of Kālī's 'opening' and 'closing'. Her world is an eternal living flux in which all things arise and all disappear again. She is the archetypal image of birth-and-death, giver of life and its destroyer, 'the vital principles of the visible universe which has many faces – gracious, cruel, creative, destructive, loving, indifferent – the endless possibility of the active energy at the heart of the world'.[26]

Kālī's origins can be traced to non-Aryan and Vedic sources. Such names as Ambikā, Durgā and Kālī begin to appear in the later Vedic texts; some scholars have suggested that the Vedic goddess Aditi is a precursor. In the view of Swami Abhedananda the Vedic goddess Rātri in the course of time became transformed into Kālī. The conception of *Kāla* – Time – as goddess can be found in the *Mahābhārata*. The name Bhadra-Kāli is first found mentioned in the Vedic hymn the *Grihya-sūtra*. The nakedness of the goddess Vāc in the *Aitareya Brāhmaṇa* may be connected with the nakedness ascribed to Kālī in later days. The *Muṇḍaka Upanishad* names Kālī and Karālī, but they are described as two of the seven tongues of Agni (the creator-god), corresponding to the Seven Divine Mothers – the Sapta Mātṛikā.

Though the Goddess is one, and there can be nothing apart from her, according to the capability and desire of the worshipper she is conceived of in innumerable forms. The *Todala Tantra* gives her well-known forms as eight, while the *Mahākālasaṃhitā* gives the nine names of the goddess Kālī as Dakshiṇa, Smashāna, Bhadra, Guhya, Kāla, Kāmakalā, Dhana, Siddhi and Caṇḍikā. The black, south-facing Dakshiṇakālī is usually depicted standing upon the recumbent form of Śiva, while the similar Smashānakālī is often shown engaged in *viparīta-rati* (sexual union in which the female partner is on top) with Śiva, a realization of non-duality in which there is no separation, no linear flow, just fullness, completeness.

The Supreme Goddess is the source of all 'energies', and the feminine divinities are principally her emanations, or her partial archetypal images. The immense array of the goddess-transformations of Kālī are classified in descending order. Certain goddesses are complete manifestations of the supreme feminine principle; some are her partial emanations; some are fractions of her power; mortal women are included as 'parts of parts of fractions' of the Supreme Goddess.

The 'knowledge' aspect of Kālī is represented by a śakti-cluster of ten goddesses known as the Daśa-Mahāvidyās, the Ten Great or Transcendental Wisdoms. The first Mahāvidyā is Kālī herself, as the power of Time, and the other forms are Tārā, the potential of re-creation; Ṣoḍaśī, 'sixteen', the power of perfection, fullness; Bhuvaneśvarī, supporter of all existence, space-consciousness; Chinnamastā, the end of existence, the distributor of life-energy; Bhairavī, the active power of destruction; Dhūmāvatī, the power of darkness, inertia; Bagalā, destroyer of negative forces; Mātaṅgī, the

Dakshiṇakālī, the 'south-facing' Kālī, energizing the inert form of Śiva beneath her feet. Bengal, c. 18th century, brass

Daśa-Mahāvidyās, the Ten Great Wisdoms, feminine energies which together encompass the entire knowledge of the universe. Below them are their consort-gods. Mithila, watercolour on paper

Badrakālī, the form of Kālī representing everything benevolent and joyful. Basohli school, 17th century, gouache and gold on paper

Opposite: Mahāvidyā Dhūmāvatī, the 'smokey one', the Kālī who reduces the universe to ashes. She represents the inert phase of the cosmic cycle, the darkness before the wheel's-turn brings the Mahāvdiyā Kamalā, the bright phase of reconstituted unity. Rajasthan, c. 18th century, gouache on paper

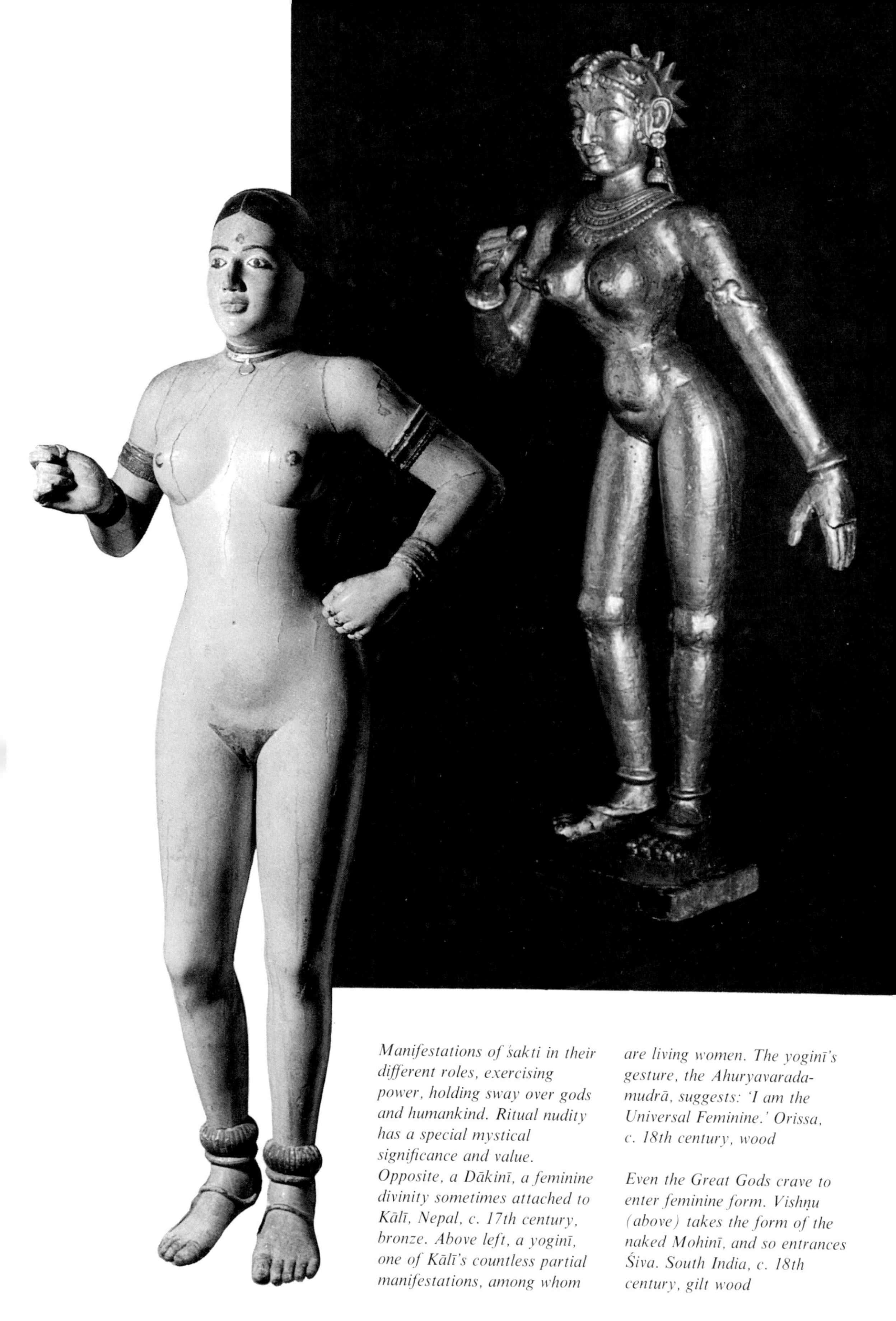

Manifestations of śakti in their different roles, exercising power, holding sway over gods and humankind. Ritual nudity has a special mystical significance and value. Opposite, a Dākinī, a feminine divinity sometimes attached to Kālī, Nepal, c. 17th century, bronze. Above left, a yoginī, one of Kālī's countless partial manifestations, among whom are living women. The yoginī's gesture, the Ahuryavarada-mudrā, suggests: 'I am the Universal Feminine.' Orissa, c. 18th century, wood

Even the Great Gods crave to enter feminine form. Vishṇu (above) takes the form of the naked Mohinī, and so entrances Śiva. South India, c. 18th century, gilt wood

power of domination, dispeller of evil; and Kamalā, the state of reconstituted unity. These nine goddesses are no longer worshipped separately from Kālī, or if they are, their cults are esoteric.

Each of the goddesses has a specific cosmic function. Together, as the power of wisdom, they awaken the worshipper to the illusion of existence. Represented in their yantra, they are the embodiments of human perfections.

Tantrism shows a preference for a dynamic concept of cosmic unity which implies a harmonization of all differentiations and paradoxes. The Śakti-cluster of the Mahāvidyās as a whole reflects this dynamic unity of existence, in which all aspects of life, the darkest, the purest, the most forceful and the inert, are combined to form a whole, a vision of unity in diversity.

Like all the Mahāvidyās, Kālī is a Great Yoginī. Though countless forms of yoginīs emerged from the body of Kālī, sixty-four of them are named in the *Kālīkā Purāṇa* with their prescribed worship, and in the *Bhūtaḍāmara* (a tantric text) eight different methods of yoginī-worship are described.

For ritual worship the yoginī is generally represented by a naked woman. Mircea Eliade comments on the significance of this nudity: 'Every naked woman incarnates *prakṛiti*. Hence she is to be looked upon with the same adoration and the same detachment that one exercises in pondering the unfathomable secret of nature, its limitless capacity to create. The ritual nudity of the *yoginī* has an intrinsic mystical value: if, in the presence of the naked woman, one does not in one's inmost being feel the same terrifying emotion that one feels before the revelation of the cosmic mystery, there is no rite, there is only a secular act, with all the familiar consequences (strengthening of the karmic chain, etc.).'[27]

Kālī's three manifestations for the creation, preservation and destruction of the universe are represented graphically in the *Kāmakalā-chidvalli*: 'The goddess of renowned form assumes, in time of protection, the form of a straight line; in time of destruction she takes the form of a circle, and for creation she takes on the brilliant appearance of a triangle.' In her yantra form, Kālī is symbolised by the central dot, bindu, the source of objectivization or womb of the world. Her unfolding is represented by the five triangles, which are the five *jñānendriyas* (organs of knowledge) and the five *karmendriyas* (motor organs); the encompassing circle, which is *avidyā* (false knowledge, i.e. knowledge of the illusory world of separate objects); and the eight-petalled lotus, which is the eight-fold Prakṛiti (Nature): earth, water, fire, air, ether, *Manas* (Mind), *Buddhi* (Intellect) and *Ahaṃkāra* (ego-consciousness). Her cosmogonic diagram is imbued with the pulsation of *prāṇas*, the life-force.

Mahākālī, the Great Goddess, with ten heads indicating her all-pervading nature. Kangra school, c. 18th century, gouache on paper

Her creative role as Prakṛiti associates Kālī with the active power of time. She represents the cyclical time-consciousness that transcends individual destiny. Kālī destroys Mahākāla at the time of Great Dissolution: that is, Kālī as the Power-of-Time absorbs Kāla (Time), the All-Destroyer. She is constantly reminding us that we cannot attain liberation so long as we remain within the relative space and time of our planet, in our universe with its billions of stars, galaxies, and nebulae, in our existence for one second of world-time compared with the absolute and eternal.

Kālī, as Durgā in her 'forceful' role, is the antagonist of all evil in the eternal cosmic struggle, yet she is herself the personification of all benign and terrible forces. Signifying a vision of the Whole, Kālī becomes the Supreme. 'He whom you call Brahman [Highest Reality], I call Śakti,' said the nineteenth-century mystic-saint Ramakrishna.

> Of my own free will have I divided my form for the purpose
> of creation into the dual aspects of male and female.
> As Brahma I create this universe of moving and
> non-moving things,
> and as Mahārudra, of my own will, I destroy it at the time
> of dissolution.
>
> *Mahābhāgavata*

Kālī is worshipped as Ādyā-Śakti, the Beginning of All. 'I am Kālī, the Primal Creative Force, as the *Śaktisaṅgama Tantra* states. After the Great Dissolution, Kālī alone remains, as Avyakta Prakṛiti (Unmanifest Nature) in a state of potential power, the Supreme Śakti, the Eternal Feminine.

5
Divine Mother

Who dares misery love,
And hug the form of death,
Dance in destruction's dance
To him the Mother comes.

Vivekananda

Śākta doctrine places the Daśa Mahāvidyās, the śakti-cluster of the Ten Great Wisdoms, at the very core of the faith. The form of Kālī worshipped in Eastern India, and particularly in Bengal, is that of the Mahāvidyā Kālī. It is she, usually represented as the black, south-facing Dakshiṇakālī, who is welcomed into the home as Divine Mother.

The worship of the image of Dakshiṇakālī is especially associated with the name of Krishnananda, author of *Tantrasāra*. Krishnananda (*c*. 1585) lived in Navadvipa, West Bengal, a leading centre of Sanskrit learning and the birthplace of a number of extraordinary personalities, supreme among them Caitanya who was regarded as an incarnation of Kṛishṇa. Kālī, however, was worshipped in Bengal long before the time of Krishnananda. Her worship was certainly well established in its present form by the fifteenth century, and by the twentieth century, community Kālī-pūjā and Durgā-pūjā were gaining ground.

In her archetypal form, Mother Kālī often has no iconographic image but is represented by a stone block or even a mound. The Chinese pilgrim Hiuen Tsang who visited the Gandhara region of the North West Frontier in the seventh century described the image of Bhīmādevī as a dark-blue stone. Kālī under the name of Guhyakālī is popular in Nepal: she resides there beside Śiva, and here, too, a block of stone is worshipped. In many of the temples of Bengal, although the goddess is called Tārā, as, for example, in the Tārā-piṭha in West Bengal, the image is of Kālī's archetypal form.

The goddess is known in Kashmir as Tripurā or Tripurasundarī, in Kerala as Kālī. Variations of Kālī's name occur throughout the ancient world. In Europe, it is said, the Greeks had a name Kalli. Their city of Kallipolis, it is suggested, is the modern Gallipoli. The

Dakshiṇakālī, the Divine Mother. Kalighat, South Calcutta, traditional image, clay

Archetypal goddess-image: a black stone. Silver-foil patch and colouring of dark-blue and crimson pastes. Rajasthan

Black Goddess was known in Finland as Kalma (Kali Ma), and gipsies 'who came originally from India' to the West still know the goddess Sara-Kali. 'Lunar priests of Sinai, formerly priestesses of the Moon-goddess, called themselves *kalu*. Similar priestesses of prehistoric Ireland were *kelles*, origin of the name Kelly, which meant a hierophanic clan devoted to "the Goddess Kele".'[28] It is interesting to note that the name of the Mother-goddess as Danu occurs in the literature of both India and Ireland.

The worship of Kālī is characterized by a fervent self-surrender to the Mother. As the anthropologist Abrahim H. Khan writes of the Kali-Mai pūjā at the Kali Temple in Guyana, South America, it is by expressions of love and faith the worshipper gains deeper religious consciousness and familiarity with his or her own true self.[29] For Aurobindo, the goddess 'mediates between the human personality and the divine Nature' and is 'the power responsible for the support of the biological, physiological, and moral processes as well. Therefore, she manifests herself not only through the laws of nature, but through the life processes, attitudes, dispositions', and the individual's 'state of bondage or liberation'.[30] Khan comments: 'To belong truly to her, the worshipper must surrender not just the intellect, but the entire self, that is, the mind and body. Every aspect of one's being must be dedicated to her service for one to become her true devotee. Only the true devotee can be conscious of the Divine Presence and can sing her song and dance her dance of life.'

X, XI *Forest Kālī with yoni-kuṇḍa in front, Bihar*

XII *Kālī as the Great Wisdom Chinnamastā, nourishing new life with the blood-nectar issuing from her severed neck. Kangra school, c. 18th century, gouache on paper*

X

XI

XII

Devotion to the goddess as a means of attaining experience of the Supreme Reality is especially exemplified in the life of Ramakrishna, the great saint of nineteenth-century India who served Mother Kālī at the Dakshinesvar Kālī Temple in North Calcutta. Ramakrishna has described how the whole current of his mind began to flow towards the Mother; how he longed to come face to face with her, and in an agony of restlessness, vowed he would kill himself unless she appeared to him. At the peak of his longing he felt, he said:

> as if someone had taken hold of my heart and mind, and was wringing them like a wet towel. My eyes fell on the sword on the wall of the Mother's temple. I made up my mind to end my life that very moment. Like one mad I ran and caught hold of it, when suddenly I had the wonderful vision of the Mother and fell down unconscious. I did not know what happened then in the external world – how that day and the next slipped away. But in my heart of hearts there was flowing a current of intense bliss, never experienced before, and I had the immediate knowledge of the light that was the Mother. It was as if houses, doors, temples, and everything else vanished from my sight, leaving no trace whatsoever. However far and in whatever direction I looked I saw a continuous succession of effulgent waves rushing at me from all sides, with great speed. I was caught on the rush, and panting for breath I collapsed unconscious.

From that time onwards, Ramakrishna perceived everything around him as full of Consciousness, as the embodiment of Spirit. The image of the Mother was Consciousness, the worship utensils were Consciousness, the altar was Consciousness, the door-sill, the marble floor, he himself – all Consciousness.

> I found everything inside the room soaked, as it were, in Bliss – the Bliss of *Sat-Cit-Ānanda* [Being-Consciousness-Bliss]. I saw an evil man in front of the Kālī Temple; but in him also I saw the power of the Divine Mother vibrating. That was why I fed a cat with the food that was to be offered to the Divine Mother, saying, 'Wilt Thou take it, Mother?' I clearly perceived that the Divine Mother Herself had become everything – even the cat.

When Ramakrishna intended to offer the Mother a flower, he found his hand coming towards his own head and placing the flower there. The very distinction between himself and the Mother had vanished. Once he prostrated himself before a prostitute-actress playing on the

XIII *Devī with sword and severed head signifying the end of one cosmic cycle, and waters flowing from the hair of Śiva representing the start of the new. Rajasthan, c. 18th century, gouache on paper*

XIV *The White Kālī (Śveta-Kālī), standing on dark Śiva. Kangra school, c. 17th century, gouache on paper*

stage of a Calcutta theatre, saying, 'Mother, have you come this time in this form?' For the Mother seems to be saying: 'A prostitute is also Myself; there is nothing except Myself.'

As his communion with the Mother began to deepen, where previously in a vision he would see a hand or a foot or the face of the Mother, now he saw her full figure, smiling, talking. Where he used to see a beam of light from her eyes, touching upon the food-offering, now he saw her actually eat the food. Where he had been seeing the living Presence *in* the image, now he saw no image, he saw the Divine Mother herself, all consciousness.

> I put the palm of my hand near Her nostrils and felt that Mother was actually breathing. I observed very closely but could never see the shadow of the Mother's divine person on the temple wall in the light of the lamp at night. I heard from my room that Mother, merry like a little girl, was going upstairs, Her anklets making jingling sounds. I came up to test it and found that She, with hair dishevelled, was actually standing on the verandah of the upper floor of the temple, looking now at Calcutta, now at the Ganges.

At this period Calcutta was rapidly becoming Anglicized, but the popularity of the Kālī Temple at Kalighat was undiminished. The city of Calcutta was built on the 'land of Kālī' (Kālī-kshetra). Legend has it that the toe of the right foot of Satī fell to earth besides the Ganges, and there the Kalighat Temple was built. Its nearby village Kalikata gave the Anglicized name Calcutta. It is suggested Calcutta's main north-south thoroughfare 'Chowringhee' was named during the British time after the ninth-century saint Chouringi-nātha who is credited with establishing the Kālī image in Kalighat, and who followed this road to worship at the Kālī Temple.

Ramakrishna's devotion to the Divine Mother attracted many disciples from the city to the Dakshinesvar Temple, one of whom, Narendra (1863–1902), was a graduate of a Christian missionary college, acquainted with Western philosophy and of a sceptical cast of mind. Narendra has described how, soon after meeting Ramakrishna in 1892, he lost his father and the family fell into economic distress.

> A firm faith arose in my mind that all the sufferings would certainly come to an end as soon as I prayed to the Mother, inasmuch as Ramakrishna (Master) said so. I waited for the night in great expectancy. The night arrived at last. Three hours of the night had elapsed when the Master asked me to go to the holy temple. As I was going, a sort of profound inebriation possessed me, I was reeling. A firm conviction gripped me that I should actually see the

Mother and hear Her words. I forgot all other things, and became completely merged in that thought alone. Coming into the temple. I saw that Mother was actually pure infinite love and beauty. My heart swelled with loving devotion; and, beside myself with bliss, I made repeated salutations to Her, praying, 'Mother grant me discrimination, grant me detachment, grant me divine knowledge and devotion; ordain that I may always have unobstructed vision of Thee.' My heart was flooded with peace. The whole universe completely disappeared and Mother alone remained filling my heart.

No sooner had I returned to the Master than he asked, 'Did you pray to Mother for the removal of your worldly wants?' Startled at his question, I said, 'No, sir; I forgot to do so. So, what should I do now?' He said, 'Go quickly again and pray to Her.' I started for the temple once more, and coming to Mother's presence, became inebriated again. I forgot everything, bowed down to Her repeatedly and prayed for the realization of divine knowledge and devotion before I came back. The Master smiled and said, 'Well, did you tell Her this time?' I was startled again and said, 'No, sir; hardly had I seen the Mother when I forgot everything on account of the influence of an indescribable divine Power and prayed for knowledge and devotion only. What's to be done now?' The Master said, 'Silly boy, could you not control yourself a little and make that prayer? Go once more, if you can, tell Her those words. Quick!' I started a third time; but as soon as I entered the temple a formidable sense of shame occupied my heart. I thought what a trifling thing I have come to ask of Mother. It is, as the Master says, just like the folly of asking a king, having received his grace, for gourds and pumpkins. Ah! how low is my intellect! Overpowered with shame and aversion I bowed down to Her over and over again saying, 'I don't want anything else, Mother; do grant me knowledge and devotion only.'

After Ramakrishna's death Narenda, now known as Swami Vivekananda, became renowned as a speaker of great spiritual power. In 1893 he was sent by the Raja of Ramnad to the Parliament of Religions in Chicago, and afterwards travelled to England and Europe where he lectured on Vedanta, gaining some notable disciples, among them an Englishwoman Margaret Noble (Sister Nivedita), author of *Kali the Mother*.

Vivekananda predicted 'the resurgence of the Mother into the consciousness of the world's population, after patriarchal religions had forced her into concealment in the unconscious'. 'One vision I see clear as life before me, that the ancient Mother has awakened once

more, sitting on her throne rejuvenated, more glorious than ever. Proclaim her to all the world with the voice of peace and benediction.'

In India, Kālī-worship received a fresh impetus during the days of the national (*swadeshi*) movement during Vivekananda's time, when the goddess was regarded as Bengal personified.

Kālī is worshipped today at pilgrimage sites from Peshwar to Assam and from Kashmir to Kanya-kumari (Cape Comorin). Modern 'kalibari' ('Homes of Kālī') have been established for community worship, with social and cultural activities centred around Kālī-pūjā and Durgā-pūjā.

Worship of the feminine principle as *kumārī*, a virgin girl, is one of the ceremonies performed during the great annual festival of Durgā and Kālī, for 'All females in all the worlds are but my parts'. Even as *kumārī*, the feminine is also Kālī. Traditionally the *kumārī* was worshipped as a naked girl – that is, stripped of the covering of Māyā. Today during the festival, young girls receive the ritual worship of their families dressed in their new clothes.

Kālī dances the cosmic dance, revealing to the girl who crouches at her feet (detail, left) the feminine grandeur of the universe. Gujarat, c. 16th century, stone

The festival worship continues for fifteen days, from the first day of the waxing moon to the full moon. The waxing and waning phases of the moon stand for the cosmic cycle of evolution and involution, extension and reabsorption. The eternal Sixteenth Part, *ṣoḍaśanityā*, the fullness of Śakti, is personified by a girl of sixteen (*ṣoḍaśī*), representing the source of all life. According to Tantra, 'by worshipping the girl, human beings submit their wills to the universe'.

Ṣoḍaśī is the name of the third of the Daśa Mahāvidyās or Ten Great Wisdoms. She is associated with Lalitā (also known as Tripurā, Tripurasundarī, Mahātripurasundarī or Rājarājeśvarī), the presiding deity of one of the most important Śakti cults, called Śrī-vidyā. The cult of Śrī-vidyā was once practised widely from Kashmir to Kerala, and more texts have been written about it than about any other. The yantra of Tripurasundarī is the famous 'Śrī-yantra' or Śrī-chakra', the power-diagram which symbolizes the universe and its divine cause.

Next to Dakshiṇakālī in popularity, Smashānakālī is the image worshipped particularly by those advanced tantrikas who practise ritual worship of the goddess in the cremation ground. Kālī, the Lady of the Dead, refuses no-one. She is ever awake at the Burning Ghāt. In her purposes she is impartial, guiding according to each individual's needs and nature, and to the circumstances, helping in adequate measure. Death is looked upon as her transforming touch that removes pain, sorrow, anxiety, and gives freedom and peace. The flickering flames of the pyre are full of compassion.

Ramakrishna once described a vision of the divine Māyā by which the universe is created and sustained, and into which it is finally absorbed. He saw an exquisitely beautiful woman, heavy with child, emerge from the Ganges, give birth, and begin tenderly to nurse her infant. A moment later, she had assumed a terrible aspect, and seizing the child in her jaws, crushed it. Devouring her offspring she re-entered the water. Mahāmāyā is the all-creating, the all-nourishing, the all-devouring.

Smashānakālī at the Burning Ghāt. From each of the goddess's ears hangs a tiny figure of a sādhaka – the child-like devotee so dear to the Mother. Her nature is liberation. Mandi school, c. 18th century, gouache on paper

6
Supreme Reality

She is Light itself and transcendent.
Emanating from Her body are rays in
thousands – two thousand, a hundred thousand,
tens of millions, a hundred million –
there is no counting their numbers.
It is by and through Her that all things moving
and motionless shine. It is by the light of
this Devī that all things become manifest.

Bhairava Yāmala

In the *Devī Upanishad* the Supreme Goddess explains her true nature, that transcends all empiric existence:

> Great Goddess, who art Thou?
>
> She replies: I am essentially Brahman [the Absolute].
> From me has proceeded the world comprising Prakṛiti [material substance]
> and Purusha [cosmic consciousness],
> the void and the Plenum.
> I am [all forms of] bliss and non-bliss.
> Knowledge and ignorance are Myself.
> I am the five elements and also what is different from them,
> the pañchabhūtas [five gross elements] and tanmātras [five subtle elements].
>
> I am the entire world.
> I am the Veda as well as what is different from it.
> I am unknown.
> Below and above and around am I.

It is the Krama system of Kashmir, a system distinct and independent, which defines the Ultimate Reality as Kālī. The Krama philosophy in Kashmir Śaivism has been elaborately expounded by Abhinavagupta (AD 950–1020), a philosopher-saint of the highest spiritual attainment.

In the Krama philosophy Kālī is called, first, Mātrisadbhāva, the free, self-luminous conscious energy, manifesting itself successively in the forms of twelve Kālīs; second, Vāmeśvarī, signifying the power of Consciousness (*Cit-śakti*), shining in everything; and third,

Kālī yantra representing the unfolding of the world of the senses, powers and appearances from Kālī symbolized by the central bindu. Rajasthan, 18th century, gouache on paper

Kālaśaṅkarṣinī, because she is not limited by time (*kāla*) which is essentially of the nature of succession, despite her successive manifestations, through all of which she remains unaffected. She is essentially of the nature of light, of consciousness and freedom.

Abhinavagupta wrote a *Krama-stotra* in praise of the twelve Kālīs, and describes them as follows:

The first, Sṛisṭhikālī, creation of objects, is the Supreme Consciousness (Parāsaṁvit) when the will to create arises in her, and the would-be creation shines in outline objectively within her.

The second, Raktakālī, experience of objects, is when, after the manifestation of the objective world, the Supreme Consciousness manifests herself as the means of knowledge (the five senses) and is affected by the externalized objective world. This is the concept of the power of 'preservation' in relation to the object.

The third, Sthitināśakālī, termination of the experience of objects, is the Supreme Consciousness intent upon terminating her extrovert form, and, therefore, the objective world, because of her inclination to rest within herself in the form of the consciousness: 'I have known the object.' This is the concept of 'annihilation' in relation to the object.

The fourth, Yamakālī, doubt about the experience of the object, is the concept of indefinable power relating to conceptual objects and experience. It leads to the rise of doubt about the objects of experience, that is present as a mere idea and to its removal or destruction.

The subtle distinction between the latter two (Sthitināśakālī and Yamakālī) is, 'I have known the object', and, 'the objects of experience are non-different from me'.

The fifth, Saṁhārakālī, dissociation of objects from external norms, centres round the power of destruction. After the destruction of doubt, or its objects, the Supreme Consciousness brings about the disappearance of the externality of the objects, and groups them within, as one with herself.

The sixth, Mṛtyukālī, total merging of object in subject, is of the nature of death (*Mṛtyu*), causing the disappearance of the externality of objects. But it is related to objectivity, in so far as it realizes objectivity as non-different from itself. But this objectivity can have being only if it rests on the Subject (*Pramātr*) that is free from all limitations. Mṛtyukālī is so called because it engulfs even Saṁhārakālī.

The seventh, Rudrākālī or Bhadrakālī, object momentarily reinstated to be finally dissolved, is when, immediately after dissolving the multitude of objects, the Universal Consciousness gives rise to a definite object in the mind of an individual subject. To this object, which is a revived mental picture of a particular action done in the past, doubt is related. The doubt about it is, whether it was right or

Kālānala yantra, symbolizing the Fire of Doom, merging Spirit with Pure Wisdom. Rajasthan, 18th century, gouache on paper

wrong. And the certainty about its being right or wrong is responsible for its fruition in the pleasant or unpleasant experiences here and hereafter.

The eighth, Mārtaṇḍakālī, merging of the twelve faculties, is Universal Consciousness, in that she brings about the merging of all the twelve means of knowledge, the *Indriyas* – which are the five senses of perception, the five organs of action, *Manas* (Mind) and *Buddhi* (Intellect) – in the *Ahaṃkāra* or ego-consciousness. Mārtaṇḍakālī represents the *Anākhya* (indefinable) power in relation to the means of knowledge, in so far as it brings about the identification of the twelve means of knowledge with the ego-consciousness, to the extent that they completely lose their being, and become unnameable.

The preceding four Kālīs are the aspects of the Universal Consciousness which destroy the means of knowledge and action. The following four, beginning with Paramārkakālī, are such as destroy the limited subject.

The ninth, Paramārkakālī, is merging of ego-consciousness into the limited subject of 'spirit'. It represents the particular power in relation to the limited subject in so far as it brings about the emergence of the limited subject through merging in it of *Ahaṃkāra*, ego-consciousness.

Kālī yantra, Nepal. (Painting after the original by Bradley A. Te Paske, Santa Fe)

The tenth, Kālānalarudrakālī, merging Spirit with Pure Wisdom, is the particular power of the Universal Consciousness when she brings about the merging of a limited self with the Universal Self, in whom all objectivity has its being. This power of the limited subject resting in the Universal is experienced as 'I am all this'. Because of her capacity for holding everything, even time, within herself, she is called Mahākālī, the Supreme Kālī.

The experience which characterizes Mahākāla (Time transcending time) is, 'I am all this'. But there is a yet higher experience, in which the 'this' element is absent. The distinction between these two experiences is that in the former the 'I' rests on the 'this', but in the latter, the 'this' being absent, the 'I' rests within itself.

The eleventh, Mahākālakālī, merging Pure Wisdom in Energy, is the Universal Consciousness as she brings about the merging of the 'I' which shines in opposition to 'this', as 'I am all this', into the 'Pure I', the 'Perfect I', the 'Akula', which is free from all relations to 'objectivity', to 'this'. Subject is annihilated here.

The twelfth, Mahābhairavacaṇḍograghorakālī, merging Energy in the Absolute, embraces 'Perfect I', 'Akula', subject, object, the means of knowledge as well as knowledge in perfect unity with Pure Consciousness.

The stage is called Parā. It does not manifest itself in subject, object, means of knowledge or knowledge, and therefore is free from all relations. It is 'total'.

The concept of the Whole is explained by Ramakrishna in simple language: 'Thus Brahman and Śakti are identical. If you accept the one, you must accept the other. It is like fire and its power to burn. If you see the fire, you must recognize its power to burn also. You cannot think of fire without its power to burn, nor can you think of the power to burn without fire. You cannot conceive of the sun's rays without the sun, nor can you conceive of the sun without its rays . . .

'Thus one cannot think of Brahman without Śakti, or of Śakti without Brahman. One cannot think of the Absolute without the Relative, or of the Relative without the Absolute.

'The Primordial Power is ever at play. She is creating, preserving, and destroying in play, as it were. This Power is called Kālī. Kālī is verily Brahman, and Brahman is verily Kālī. It is one and same Reality. When we think of It as inactive, that is to say, not engaged in the acts of creation, preservation and destruction, then we call It Brahman. But when It engages in these activities, then we call It Kālī or Śakti. The Reality is one and the same; the difference is in name and form.'

7
Kalighat Paintings

Kalighat paintings are the work of Bengali folk-artists (called *patuās*) who lived in a settlement around the Kālī Temple of Kalighat, South Calcutta, from the early nineteenth century. Alongside the usual themes of the temple deity and mythological subjects, these *patuās* painted family reunions, popular amusements, and other such scenes of everyday life. Themes such as drunkenness, domestic quarrels, religious hypocrisy, feminine power, are developed in short series of pictures designed to be sold to the pilgrims and general public who flocked to the temple.

All the great temples of India have their settlements of artists and craftsmen, but it is only at Kalighat that the artists' work includes elements of social satire, even themes of social revolt. The directness and truthfulness of the subject-matter is matched by the bold style.

Yet Kalighat pictures, like all temple paintings, are virtually collective creations, the products of several members of a family with generations of artist behind them. The sense of the whole is always present in the mind of the painter. The family system gave security, without which the artists could not have developed their work in close touch with tradition. If the opportunity for a radical assertion of individuality in the modern sense was very limited, the common style is linear, simplified and rhythmical, and the colourings are bold. Even when the brushstrokes tend to be stylized, as a result of repetition over the years, Kalighat paintings retain the vitality of traditional colour-combinations. The predominant colours are lampblack, ochre, orpiment, indigo, green. Silver colour is used for outlines such as those of the body beneath clinging garments, or ornaments, cushions, etc. The *patuās* painted with colloid of tin, which was cheap, and unlike silver, did not lose its lustre after burnishing. Modelling of form was done with darker tones applied to a wet paper-surface.

Composition is simple. Most of the paintings depict just one or two figures; every figure is portrayed in a way that the *patuās* regarded as basic, simplifying the outlines of the body or even arranging them as

Kālī. Patuā painting. Kalighat school, South Calcutta, 19th century, watercolour on paper

A wife leads her sheepish husband by a string. Above right, Bhairavī tramples a male figure underfoot. Kalighat school, 19th century, watercolour on paper

patterns. The best specimens of Kalighat art are colourful paintings or black-and-white drawings with a joyous, impetuous line.

One of the series of pictures ridicules men's foolish nature and bad habits, a popular theme in Bengali folk-literature, while another notable group expresses woman's assertiveness. A man is depicted as a lamb whom a woman leads on a string, or the woman's dominant position is indicated by her trampling of the male, recalling Kālī's trampling on Śiva. The sense of woman's freedom and power is strong. W.G. Archer commented on the man-lamb: 'We are reminded of a mother-in-law's joking admonitions to the bridegroom at weddings in Bengal: "I have purchased you with cowries. I have tied you with a rope. I have put a spindle in your hand. Now bleat like a sheep." But it is not the sheep-husband but the sheep-lover who sustains this vapid role.' Archer observes that 'such pictures may well have been influenced by dim associations with the goddess Kālī and may even, in some oblique way, have glorified the "female principle".'[31]

Though the last representatives of the Kalighat school of painters are dead, and Kalighat paintings are to be seen only in the collections of museums such as the Asutosh Museum, Calcutta, the Victoria and Albert Museum,[32] London, the Pushkin Museum, Moscow, and the Napistek Museum, Prague, the association between women's freedom and independence and Kālī is one certain to be seen in the future.

XV *Western vision of Kālī, Kali Yuga Exhibition, San Francisco, 1986. Painting by Maitreya Bowen. Oil and gold leaf on cardboard*

XVI *Temple-image of Kālī worshipped at Kalighat, South Calcutta, stone*

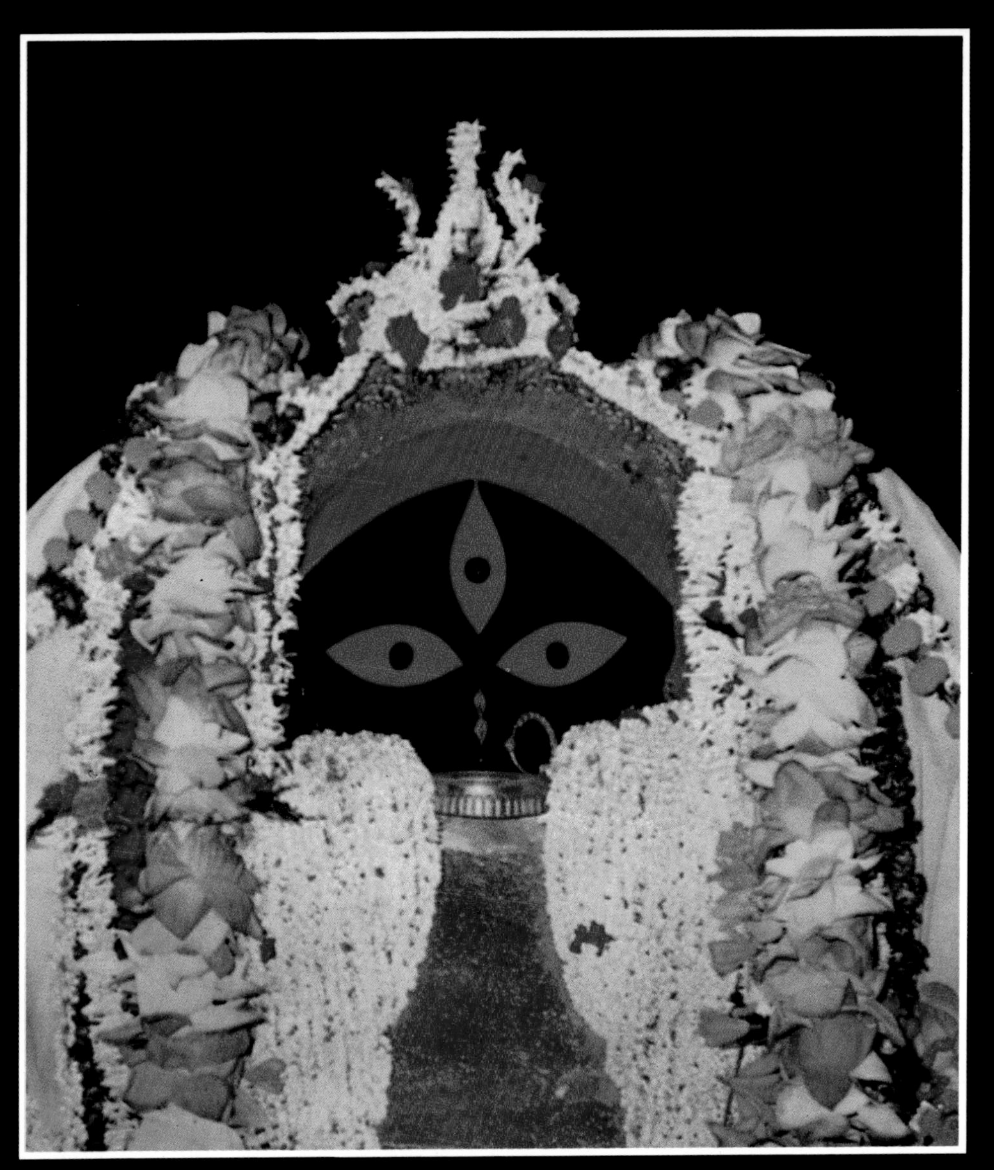

XVI

জয়কালী ক্লথ প্রিন্টিং ওয়ার্কস

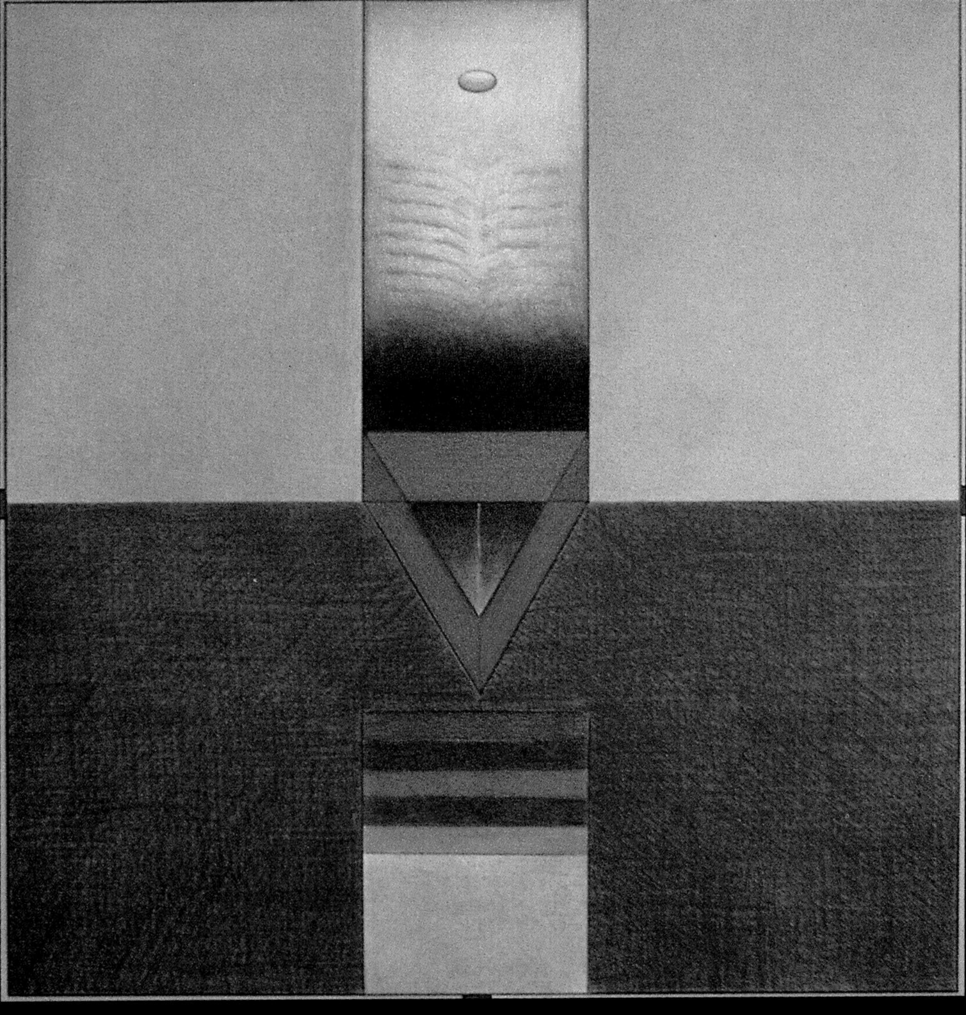

XVIII

8
Hymns to Kālī

That power who exists in all beings as Peace,
reverence to Her, reverence to Her, reverence to Her,
reverence, reverence.

Devī-Māhātmya

The hymns to Kālī express the praise of her endless forms, though She is One. She exists in all that is, animate and inanimate, for the universe with all its diverse manifestations is but her parts. All life and beings are to be worshipped as herself, in verse and song.

The vast Śākta literature contains many poems to illustrate the goddess's 'world-play' (*līlā*), the realization of which dispels all fear. For the Mother is only terrible to those who are living in the illusion of separateness; who have not yet realized their unity with her, and known that all her forms are for enlightenment.

In the *Devī-Māhātmya*, recited during the festival of Durgā, one of the hymns recited proclaims the Goddess's all-pervading power:

That power who is defined as Consciousness in all beings,
reverence to Her, reverence to Her, reverence to Her,
reverence, reverence.

That power who is known as Reason in all beings,
reverence to Her, reverence to Her, reverence to Her,
reverence, reverence.

That power who exists in all beings in the form of Sleep,
reverence to Her, reverence to Her, reverence to Her,
reverence, reverence.

That power who exists in all beings as Hunger,
reverence to Her, reverence to Her, reverence to Her,
reverence, reverence.

That power who exists in all beings as Shadow,
reverence to Her, reverence to Her, reverence to Her,
reverence, reverence.

XVII *Mask of Tārā, a popular name of Kālī. West Bengal, brass*

XVIII *Contemporary vision of Kālī as 'Preserver'. Coloured pencils on paper, Priya Mookerjee, New York*

That power who exists in all beings as Energy,
reverence to Her, reverence to Her, reverence to Her,
reverence, reverence.

That power who exists in all beings in the form of Thirst,
reverence to Her, reverence to Her, reverence to Her,
reverence, reverence.

That power who exists in all beings as Forgiveness,
reverence to Her, reverence to Her, reverence to Her,
reverence, reverence.

That power who exists in all beings in the form of Species,
reverence to Her, reverence to Her, reverence to Her,
reverence, reverence.

That power who exists in all beings as Bashfulness,
reverence to Her, reverence to Her, reverence to Her,
reverence, reverence.

That power who exists in all beings as Peace,
reverence to Her, reverence to Her, reverence to Her,
reverence, reverence.

That power who exists in all beings in the form of Faith,
reverence to Her, reverence to Her, reverence to Her,
reverence, reverence.

That power who exists in all beings as Loveliness,
reverence to Her, reverence to Her, reverence to Her,
reverence, reverence.

That power who exists in all beings as Fortune,
reverence to Her, reverence to Her, reverence to Her,
reverence, reverence.

That power who exists in all beings as Vocation,
reverence to Her, reverence to Her, reverence to Her,
reverence, reverence.

That power who exists in all beings in the form of Memory,
reverence to Her, reverence to Her, reverence to Her,
reverence, reverence.

That power who exists in all beings as Compassion,
reverence to Her, reverence to Her, reverence to Her,
reverence, reverence.

That power who exists in all beings as Fulfilment,
reverence to Her, reverence to Her, reverence to Her,
reverence, reverence.

That power who exists in all beings as Mother,
reverence to Her, reverence to Her, reverence to Her,
reverence, reverence.

That power who exists in all beings in the form of Illusion,
reverence to Her, reverence to Her, reverence to Her,
reverence, reverence.

Though Kālī is eternal, immanent, she incarnates herself in special forms to establish divine principles. In the hymn *Ādyākālī*, Primordial Kālī, of the *Mahānirvāṇa Tantra*, she is addressed as:

Hrīm, O destroyer of time!
Srīm, O terrific one!
Krīm, Thou who art beneficent!

Possessor of all the arts,
Thou art Kamalā,
Destroyer of the pride of the Kali Age . . .

Mother of Time
Thou art brilliant as the fires
of the final dissolution.

Merciful,
Vessel of mercy,
Whose mercy is without limit,
Who art attainable alone by Thy mercy.
Who art fire,
Tawny,
Black of hue,
Thou who increaseth the joy of the Lord of creation,
Night of darkness,
Yet liberator from the bonds of desire,
Thou who art dark as a bank of cloud,
And bearest the crescent moon,
Destroyer of sin in the Kali Age,
Thou who art pleased by the worship of virgins,
Thou who art the refuge of the worshippers of virgins,
Who art pleased by the feasting of virgins,
And who art in the form of the virgin,

Traditional worship of Durgā performed in the home, Kerala

Destroyer of fear,
Who assumeth all forms at will,
Whose abode is at Kāmarūpa [Assam],
Who ever dallies at the Kāmapiṭha,
O Beautiful One,
O creeper which givest every desire,
Whose beauty is Thy ornament,
Adorable as the image of all tenderness,
Thou with a tender body,
And who art slender of waist,
Who art pleased with the nectar of consecrated wine.

Joyous one,
Revealer of the path of the Kaulikas [Kashmir Tantrikas],
Queen of Kāśi [Banaras],
Allayer of sufferings,

To Thee I make obeisance.

In the *Karpūrādi-stotra* the hymn is to Mother Kālī as Dakshiṇakālīkā, the form of the Devī most widely worshipped at the present time:

> *O Mother, Thou givest birth to and protectest the world, and at the time of dissolution dost withdraw to Thyself the earth and all things; therefore Thou art Brahmā, and the Lord of the Three Worlds, the spouse of Śrī, and Maheśa, and all other beings and things. How, then, shall I praise Thy greatness?*
>
> *Obeisance: To Kālī the spouse of Kāla [Time] who destroys all sin and is Kāla. She who is Tārā the saviour, the Supreme Brahmavidyā, who is adored by the Lotus-born Deva [Brahmā].*
>
> *She who is Śrīvidyā, desirous of the welfare of sādhakas on the path of liberation, to whom Hari [Vishṇu] and Hara [Śiva] make obeisance.*
>
> *May that Devī the Mother, who appears in the form of all things, bring forth benefits for all who sing Her praises.*

It is in Bengal that the worship of Durgā and Kālī are perhaps most deeply rooted. The Śākta songs are at the heart of the Bengali people.

The great mystic poet Ramprasad was an ardent devotee of Mother Kālī. He was born not far from Calcutta in 1718, and his fame was established in his lifetime. More than two centuries have passed since the crowd stood with him in villages and at the Ganges-side, listening to his songs for the Mother Kālī. Tradition has it that on the night of his death Ramprasad composed a song, and that as he sang the last words of it he said 'It is achieved', and so died.

Tārā, do you remember me any more?
Mother I have lived happy, is there happiness hereafter?

Had there been any other place, I could not have
besought you. But now, Mother, having given me hope,
you have cut my bonds, you have lifted me to the tree's top.

Ramprasad says: My mind is firm, and my gift
to the priest well made. Mother, my Mother, my all is
finished. I have offered my gift.

Edward J. Thompson who translated Ramprasad's songs described how he had heard them sung by 'coolies on the road, or workers in the paddy fields . . . by broad rivers at sunset, when the parrots were flying to roost and the village folk thronging from marketing to the ferry. . . . The peasants and the pundits enjoy his songs equally. They draw solace from them in the hour of despair and even at the moment of death. The dying man brought to the banks of the Ganges asks his companions to sing Ramprasadi songs.'[33]

There are many legends about Ramprasad. For instance there is the story that on his way to the Ganges to bathe he met a woman who asked him to sing to her. He told her to await his return at his home. When he asked for her, she had gone, but she had left a note for him in the family temple. It told him that the goddess Kālī had come from Kāśi (Banaras) to hear him sing, and now commanded him to come there. He set out, but fell ill twice on the way and saw a vision of Kālī telling him to forgo the journey. He composed the song:

What have I to do with Kāśi? The lotus-feet of
Kālī are place of pilgrimage enough for me.
Deep in my heart's lily meditating on them, I
float in an ocean of bliss. In Kālī's name,
where is there place for sin? When the head is not,
headache cannot remain. As when fire consumes a
pile of cotton, so all goes, in Kālī's name.

The worshipper of Kālī laughs at the name of Gayā, and at ancestral offerings there, and the story of salvation by ancestor's merits. Certainly, Śiva has said that if a man dies at Kāśi he gains salvation. But devotion is the root of everything, and salvation but her handmaid who follows her. What is the worth of salvation if it means absorption, the mixing of water with water? I love to eat sugar, but I have no wish to become sugar.

Prasad says joyously: By the power of grace and mercy, if we but think on the Wild-Locked Goddess, the Four Goods become ours.

In another song the goddess plays life's game: the kite released is the soul freed.

In the market place of this world,
The Mother sits flying Her kite.
In a hundred thousand,
She cuts the string of one or two.
And when the kite soars up into the Infinite
Oh how She laughs and claps her hands!

Ramprasad regrets neglected opportunity:

Mind, you do not know how to farm. Your fields remain untilled; had you but sown, a golden harvest had waved. Now make of Kālī's name a fence, that the crops may not be destroyed. Not Death himself (O my Mind!) dares come near this fence, your long-haired fortress. Today or after a hundred centuries – you know not when forfeiture will come. To your hand is the present time, Mind (O my Mind!). Hasten to make harvest! Scatter now the seed your teachers gave you, and sprinkle it with the water of love.

And if alone (O my Mind!) you cannot do this, then take Ramprasad with you.

Ramprasad has left the sleep of ignorance behind him, and is forever awake:

From the land where there is no night
Has come One unto me.
And night and day are now nothing to me.
Ritual worship has become forever barren.

My sleep is broken. Shall I ever sleep more?
Call it what you will – I am awake –
Hush! I have given back sleep unto Him whose it was.
Sleep have I put to sleep forever.

The music has entered the instrument,
And of that mode I have learned a song.
Ah! that music is playing ever before me,
For concentration is the great teacher thereof.
Prasad speaks: Understand, O Soul, these words of wisdom.

Later Śākta poetry follows the style of Ramprasad, with more than a dozen poets contributing to the songs of the Mother. Some of the authors of these songs are Muslims and Westerners who came to India before the arrival of the British. One, Saiyad Jafar, composed the plaint:

Why do you in such a plight call yourself merciful?
(This is the Mother, the merciful, and in such a plight!)
What wealth can you give me? You yourself have not even clothes.
Would a woman choose nakedness if she had anything with which to clothe herself?
Your husband is a beggar from his birth, your father is most cruel,
There is not in the family of either
any to be a benefactor.
For Saiyad Jafar what wealth is there in your keeping?
Hara's [Śiva's] breast possesses your twin Feet.

A Portuguese, Antony Feringhee (a general title applied to Westerners in the early days in Bengal), became an ardent devotee of Mother Kālī. He fell in love with a Bengali widow named Saudamini (or Nirupama), and lived with her in the Kālī Temple in central Calcutta, now known as the Feringhee-Kālī Temple, composing and singing *Śyāmā-saṅgīta* – songs devoted to Kālī.

Oh my Mother, would you now be kind to me?
But, when really have you shown favour to people?
Ye, Śyāmā, you have been so cruel
To Śiva, by making him flee from golden Kāśi [Banaras]
And take shelter in the burning-ground
Only to become a mendicant.

Virgin Kālī, Kalighat, South Calcutta. Watercolour on paper

Besides hymns and songs, there is some modern prose writing centred around the goddess Kālī of Calcutta's Kalighat Temple. Once, this great pilgrim-centre stood on the Ādi-Gaṅgā (the main Ganges River) noted for tidal waves. At the time of the new and full moon mountain-high bores used to run upriver and even touch the landing-steps. Sailing ships from abroad would anchor here. Today the course of the main Ganges has moved far away from the Temple of the Mother. The Ganges itself is dead, little more than a canal. But river, tree, the famous cremation ground, all remain. A Bengali novelist, Avadhut, a renunciate living in the cremation ground, has written in his *Kalitīrtha Kālighāt* (Kālīghāt, Pilgrim-centre of the Kali Age) a moving description of the Ganges there:

She is dead. So be it. Once she was Gaṅgā.
At one time she was living, and she
carried away so many thousands of bodies,
so many dead. Now, she herself is dead. So be it.
She is free. For so long she used to
liberate others; it is her own turn now.
It is good in a way.

Here at the ghāt of the old cremation ground, one can sense the eternal cry:

Dark, mute, hideous, grey, colourless,
suppressed, inaudible, incomprehensible.
It can be felt at the heart.
It is not like weeping in sadness.
It carries no tinge of sorrow, nor any pang . . .

In the midst of that dark cry, surges forth the Mother's song:

I love that Dark Beauty,
With the ruffled hair, enticing the world.
So I love her.

This black darling resides in the heart
of Mahādev [Śiva], the god of all gods.
Again Kṛishṇa the Dark
is the very life of the Brajaland (Vrindāvan),
engrossed with cowgirls there.
Hence I love black, I adore it.

Banamālī Krishṇa became the Black goddess, Kālī,
So says Prasad [Ramprasad], making no distinction
between the two.

So I love the dark beauty
Śyāmā, the heart's throb, the ruffled hair,
I love and adore her.

In the hymns and songs, the omnipotent Mother reveals her splendour and glory, her powers and her might, her magnetic and healing touch, revivifying human life. Her presence in one's heart is rapture. Like the rays of the sun, her grace and compassion flow spontaneously. Held in her gaze, one's soul is captive, and oneself in unending bliss.

'The Black Darling'. Kālī as Kāla, Great Time, dancing the cosmic dance on the breast of Eternity. Mandi school, c. 18th century, gouache on paper

Mother, I shall weave a chain of pearls for thy neck with my tears of sorrow.
The stars have wrought their anklets of light to deck thy feet, but mine will hang upon thy breast.

Wealth and fame come from thee and it is for thee to give or to withhold them. But this my sorrow is absolutely mine own,
And when I bring it to thee as my offering thou rewardest me with thy grace.

Rabindranath Tagore

Kali the Mother

The stars are blotted out,
Clouds are covering clouds,
It is darkness, vibrant, sonant.
In the roaring whirling wind
Are the souls of a million lunatics,
Just loose from the prison house,
Wrenching trees by the roots,
Sweeping all from the path.
The sea has joined the fray,
And swirls up mountain-waves,
To reach the pitchy sky.
The flash of lurid light
Reveals on every side
A thousand, thousand shades
Of Death begrimed and black –
Scattering plagues and sorrows,
Dancing mad with joy,
Come, Mother. Come!

For Terror is Thy name,
Death is in Thy breath,
And every shaking step
Destroys a world for e'er.
Thou 'Time', the All-Destroyer!
Come, O Mother. Come!

Who dares misery love,
And hug the form of Death,
Dance in destruction's dance,
To him the Mother comes.

Vivekananda

NOTES ON THE TEXT

1 Léonie Caldecott, 'The Dance of the Woman Warrior' in *Walking on the Water. Women Talk About Spirituality*, ed. Jo Garcia and Sara Maitland, London 1983, pp. 11–12.
2 Richard Shears and Isobel Gidley, *Devi the Bandit Queen*, Winchester, Mass., and London, 1984.
3 J.M. Kenoyar, J.D. Clark, J.N. Pal and G.R. Sharma, 'An Upper Palaeolithic Shrine in India', *Antiquity*, LVII, 1983, p. 89.
4 Ann Belford Ulanov, *The Feminine in Jungian Psychology and in Christian Theology*, Evanston 1971.
5 D.C. Sircar, *The Śākta Pīṭhas*, Delhi 1973.
6 *Man*. No. 129, 1932.
7 *Rig Veda*, 7, 10, 4.
8 *Rig Veda*, 8, 47, 9.
9 *Rig Veda*, X, 127.
10 *Rig Veda*, X, 125.
11 Jitendra Nath Bannerjee, 'Some Aspects of Śakti Worship in Ancient India', *Bulletin of the Ramakrishna Mission Institute of Culture*, 1953.
12 Gopi Nath Kaviraj, 'Śākta Philosophy', *History of Philosophy, Eastern and Western*, ed. S. Radhakrishnan, p. 402.
13 *Devī-Māhātmya* or *Durgā-saptasatī* (popularly known as *Caṇḍi*), from the *Mārkaṇḍeya Purāṇa*.
14 Translated by Jaideva Singh, *Spanda Kārikās. The Divine Pulsation*.
15 Ann Belford Ulanov, op. cit., p. 176.
16 *The Yonitantra*, ed. J.A. Shoterman, Banaras 1972.
17 Ann Belford Ulanov, op. cit., p. 176.
18 Stella Kramrisch, 'An Image of Aditi-uttānapād', *Artibus Asiae*, XIX, p. 259.
19 H.D. Sankalia, 'The Nude Goddess or "Shameless Woman" in Western Asia, India and South Eastern Asia.' *Artibus Asiae*, XIX, pp. 111–23.
20 Stella Kramrisch, *The Presence of Siva*, Princeton University Press, 1981, pp. 242–3.
21 *Devī-Māhātmya*, op. cit.
22 M. Esther Harding, *Woman's Mysteries, Ancient and Modern*, New York 1976, p. 125.
23 *Devī-Māhātmya*, op. cit.
24 C.G. Jung, *The Spirit in Man, Art and Literature*, London 1966.
25 Two important Sanscrit manuscripts concerning White Kālī have recently been discovered in the collection of the Asiatic Society of Bengal, Calcutta.
26 Leonard Nathan and Clinton Seely, *Grace and Mercy in Her Wild Hair*, Boulder 1982.
27 Mircea Eliade, *Le Yoga: liberté et immortalité*, Paris, 1954.
28 Barbara G. Walker, *The Woman's Encyclopedia of Myths and Secrets*, London, San Francisco 1983.
29 Abrahim H. Khan, 'Kali-Mai Puja in Guyana: Religious Function and Affirmation' in *Religion*, vol. 7, Spring 1977, p. 40.
30 Śrī Aurobindo, *The Mother*, Birth Centenary Library, Pondicherry 1972, pp. 20–2.
31 W.G. Archer, *Kalighat Paintings*, London 1971.
32 The writer Rudyard Kipling presented to the Victoria and Albert Museum, London, in 1917 a series of Kalighat paintings collected by his father, and these form the basis of the largest collection in the world.
33 Edward J. Thompson and Arthur Marshman Spencer (tr), *Bengali Religious Lyrics, Śākta*, Calcutta 1923.

PLATE ACKNOWLEDGMENTS

Archaeological Survey of India, New Delhi, 10; 12 top, centre and bottom left; 13–16; 23 bottom; 28 right; 29–31, 34, 46, 62 above. Asutosh Museum, Calcutta, 67 left. Alvin O. Bellak collection, Philadelphia, 64 below. Daniel Benveniste collection, San Francisco, XIII. C.L. Bharany collection, New Delhi, 9; 23 top; 27, 51–8, 69. Bharat Kala Bhavan collection, Banaras, V. British Library, London, 32 right. The Brooklyn Museum, New York, O. Augustus Healy and Frank L. Babbott Fund, 36. J.C. Ciancimino collection, London, 107. Crafts Museum, Calcutta, 70. Collection the late Villiers David, London, 90. Serena and Barry Dossenko collection, Butte, N. Dakota, 60. Photograph courtesy of the late Robert Fraser, London, 42 right. Musée d'Ethnographie, Geneva. IV. Photograph Robin Hamilton, London, XVI, XVII, 105. Pupul Jayakar collection, New Delhi, 64 above. Photograph Madhu Khanna, London, 22 below; 32 left; VIII–XI. Photograph Allyson P. Kneib, San Diego, I. Stella Kramrisch collection, Philadelphia (photograph Sunil Janah, Calcutta), 63. Los Angeles County Museum of Art, from the Nasli and Alice Heeramaneck Collection, Museum Associates Purchase, 43 right. Barry Miller collection 21, XIV. Ajit Mookerjee collection, 12 bottom right; II, III, 26; 33 left; 35 below; 44; 47 below; 62 below; 65–6, 84, 87. Photographs Priya Mookerjee, New York, cover; 2; 22 top; 47 above; 72, XVIII. Metropolitan Museum of Art, New York, Purchase Lita Annenburg Hazen Charitable Trust Gift, in honour of Cynthia Hazen and Leon Bernard Polsky (1982), 45. National Museum, New Delhi, 82. Thomas Neurath collection, 43 left. Lennart Nilsson, Stockholm, 42. Maurie D. Pressman collection, Philadelphia (photograph Priya Mookerjee), XVIII. Private collection, I; 35 top, XII. Robert Ravicz, Los Angeles, 59, 67 right. Franco Maria Ricci collection, Milan, 24. Fine Arts Gallery, San Diego Museum, California, anonymous loan, 80–1. Arturo Schwarz collection, Milan, 28 left. Photograph Pepita Seth, London, VI, VII, 101. R.C. Sharma collection, Jaipur, 33 right. Victoria and Albert Museum, London, 92. Photograph Ewald Weigle, Stuttgart, 35 top.

BIBLIOGRAPHY

SANSKRIT SOURCES

Rig Veda: Devī-sūkta, Rātri-sūkta, Srīsūkta (hymns)
Atharva Veda
Aitareya Brāhmaṇa
Satapatha Brāhamaṇa
Āraṇyaka: *Durgā-sūkta*

Devī Upanishad
Kaula Upanishad
Kena Upanishad
Muṇḍaka Upanishad
Praśna Upanishad
Śākta Upanishad
Sarasvatī Upanishad
Sītā Upanishad
Śvetāśvatara Upanishad
Tripuratāpini Upanishad

Mahābhārata
Rāmāyaṇa

Bhagavadgītā

Agni Purāṇa
Bhāgavata Purāṇa
Bhavishya Purāṇa
Brahmāṇḍa Purāṇa
Brahmavaivarta Purāṇa
Devībhāgavata Purāṇa
Kālīkā Purāṇa
Kūrma Purāṇa
Liṅga Purāṇa
Matsya Purāṇa
Padma Purāṇa
Skanda Purāṇa

Bhūtaḍāmara
Gandharva Tantra
Gautama Tantra
Kālī Tantra
Kāmākhayā Tantra
Kubjikā Tantra
Kulārṇava Tantra
Kumārī Tantra
Lakshmī Tantra
Lalitā-sahasranāma
Mahānirvāṇa Tantra
Meru Tantra
Nila Tantra
Niruttara Tantra
Nirvāṇa Tantra
Pañcarātra
Śaktisaṅgama Tantra
Sarvollāsa Tantra
Saundarya-laharī
Śiva Tantra
Ṣoḍaśī Tantra
Syāmā-rahasya
Tantracuḍāmanī
Tantrasāra
Todala Tantra
Vāmaṇa Tantra
Uttara Tantra
Yonitantra

OTHER SOURCES

AGRAWALA, Vasudeva S., *Devī-Māhātyam* (*The Glorification of the Great Goddess*), Varanasi 1963.
ARCHER, W.G., *Kalighat Paintings*, London 1971.
AVALON, Arthur (see also Sir John Woodroffe), *Hymns to the Goddess*, Madras 1963.
—, *Śakti and Śākta*, Madras, 1975.
BANERJEE, Jitendra Nath, *Paurāṇic and Tantric Religion*, Calcutta 1966.
BHATTACHARYA, Chakreswar, *Śāktadarśanam* (Sanskrit), Gauhati, n.d.
BHATTACHARYA, Narendra Nath, *History of the Śākta Religion*, New Delhi 1974.
BROWN, C. Mackenzie, *God as Mother: A Feminine Theology in India (An Historical and Theological Study of the Brahmavaivarta Purāṇa)*, Vermont 1974.
DALY, Mary, *Beyond God the Father*, Boston 1973.
DANIÉLOU, Alain, *Hindu Polytheism*, London and New York 1964.
DAS, H., *Tantrism: Cult of the Yoginis*, New Delhi 1980.
DAS, Upendrakumar, *Bhāratīya Śaktisādshanā*, vols I and II (in Bengali) Calcutta, Bengali date 1373.
DASGUPTA, Sashibhusan, *Bhārater Śakti-sādhanā-O-Śākta-Sāhitya* (in Bengali), Calcutta, Bengali date 1367.
DIKSHIT, S.K., *The Mother Goddess (A Study in the Origin of Hinduism)*, Poona, n.d.
GUPTA, Sanjukta, *Lakṣmī Tantra*, Leiden 1972.
HARDING, M. Esther, *Woman's Mysteries, Ancient and Modern*, New York 1976.
Hayagrīva's Śākta-Darśana (ed. K.V. ABHYANKAR), Poona 1966.
JAGADISWARANANDA, Swami (tr.), *Devī Māhatmyām*, Madras 1953.
KAVIRAJ, Gopi Nath, *Tantric Vāṅmaya me Śākta Dṛṣti* (documentation of the Śākta literature in Hindi), Patna 1963.
KHAN, Abrahim H., 'Kali-Mai Puja in Guyana' in *Religion*, Vol. VII, Spring 1977, London, pp. 35–45.
KHANNA, Madhu, *Yantra*, London and New York 1979.
KINSLEY, David R., *The Sword and the Flute*, Berkeley 1975.
KNÍKOVÁ, Hana, *The Drawings of the Kālīghāt Style*, Prague 1975.
KOSAMBI, D.D., *The Culture and Civilization of Ancient India in Historical Outlines*, London, 1965.
KRAMRISCH, Stella, 'The Indian Great Goddess' in *History of Religions*, 14, 1975, pp. 235–65.
LAHIRI, Bela, 'Śakti Cult and Coins in North-Eastern India' in *The Śakti Cult and Tārā*, ed. D.C. Sircar, Calcutta 1967, pp. 34–9.
LAL, Shyam Kishore, *Female Divinities in Hindu Mythology and Ritual*, Puna 1980.
Lalitā-Sahasranāman – Bhāskararāya's Commentary (tr. R.A., SASTRY), Madras 1970.
MAHALINGAM, T.V., 'The Cult of Śakti in Tamilnad' in *The Śakti Cult and Tārā*, ed. D.C. Sircar, Calcutta 1967, pp. 2–33.
MAJUMDAR, P.K., 'Śakti Worship in Rajasthan in *The Śakti Cult and Tārā*, ed. D.C. Sircar, Calcutta 1967, pp. 92–100.
MALLIK, Kalyani, *History and Philosophy of the Nātha Sect* (in Bengali), Calcutta 1950.
MARSHALL, Sir John, *Mohenjo-Daro and the Indus Civilization*, 3 vols., London 1931.
MAZUMDAR, B.C., 'Durga: Her Origin and History' in *Journal of the Royal Asiatic Society of Great Britain*, 38, 1906–7, pp. 355–8.
MOOKERJEE, Ajit, *Kundalinī*, London and New York 1982.
—, *Ritual Art of India*, London and New York 1985.
—, and Madhu Khanna, *The Tantric Way*, London and New York 1977.
NATHAN, Leonard, and Clinton SEELY, *Grace and Mercy in Her Wild Hair* (Selected Poems to the

Mother Goddess by Ramprasad Sen), Boulder 1982.
NEUMANN, E. *The Great Mother* (tr. Ralph Manheim), New York 1961.
PAL, Pratapaditya, *Hindu Religion and Iconography According to Tantrasāra*, Los Angeles 1981.
PANDEY, Kanti Chandra, *Abhinavagupta*, Varanasi 1963.
PARGITER, F.E. (tr.), *Mārkaṇḍeya Purāṇa*, Calcutta 1899.
PAYNE, Ernest A., *The Śāktas: An Introductory and Comparative Study*, Calcutta/London 1933.
ROY, Radharaman, '*Chit-dākāter Chittesvarī*' (in Bengali) in *Desh*, 14 July 1984, Calcutta.
SHANKARANARAYANAN, S., *Glory of the Divine Mother (Devīmāhātmyam)*, Pondicherry 1968.
SHARMA, Puspendra Kumar, *Śakti and Her Episodes on the Basis of Ancient Indian Tradition and Mythology*, Delhi 1981.
SHOTERMAN, J.A. (ed.), *The Yonitantra*, Banaras 1972.
SINHA, Jadunath (tr.), *Ram Prasad's Devotional Songs (The Cult of Shakti)*, Calcutta 1966.
SIRCAR, D.C., *The Śākta Pīṭhas*, Delhi 1973.
SISTER NIVEDITA, *Kali The Mother*, Almora 1953.
Śrī Śrī Kālī Kalpataru, ed. R. SHUKAL, Allahabad, n.d.
Śrī Śrī Kālī-pūjā-padddhati (Sanscrit in Bengali script), ed. G. VIDYANIDHI BHATTACHARYA, Calcutta, Bengali date 1385.
SWAHANANDA, Swami, *Hindu Mythology and Other Essays*, Madras 1983.
Swami Vivekananda in East and West, ed. Swami GHANANANDA and Geoffrey PARRINDER, London 1968.
THOMPSON, Edward J., and Arthur Marshman SPENCER (tr.), *Bengali Religious Lyrics, Śākta*, Calcutta 1923.
ULANOV, Ann Belford, *The Feminine in Jungian Psychology and in Christian Theology*, Evanston 1971.
VAN KOOIJ, K.R., *Worship of the Goddess According to the Kālikāpurāṇa* (Part I), Leiden 1972.
WALKER, Barbara G., *The Woman's Encyclopedia of Myths and Secrets*, San Francisco 1983.
WHITMONT, Edward C., *Return of the Goddess*, New York 1982.
WOODROFFE, Sir John (pen name Arthur Avalon, q.v.), *Hymns to Kali*, Madras 1965.
—, *Kāma-Kalā-vilāsa*, Madras 1953.
Ymmes à la Déesse, tr. Ushā P. SHĀSTRĪ and Nicole MÉNANT. Iconographic commentary C.B. Pandey. Paris 1980.

INDEX

Page numbers in italics refer to captions to plates